YORK NOTES

York Notes Rapid Revision

Lord of the Flies

AQA GCSE English Literature

Written by Beth Kemp

YORK PRESS
322 Old Brompton Road, London SW5 9JH

PEARSON EDUCATION LIMITED
80 Strand, London, WC2R 0RL

10 9 8 7 6 5 4 3 2 1

ISBN 978–1–2922–7091–3

Phototypeset by Kamae Design
Printed in Slovakia

Text credit:

Excerpts from *Lord of the Flies* (Penguin Great Books of the 20th Century) by William Golding, copyright 1954, renewed © 1982 by William Gerald Golding. Used by permission of G.P. Putnam's sons, an imprint of Penguin Publishing Group, a division of Penguin Random House LLC, all rights reserved, and with kind permission of Faber and Faber Ltd

Photo credits:

Everett Collection Historical/Alamy for page 4 top / Gino Santa Maria/Shutterstock for pages 6 middle and 44 middle / Cottonboozt/Shutterstock for pages 8 bottom and 52 middle / Gilmanshin/ Shutterstock for page 10 bottom / yellowsarah/© iStock for pages 12 middle and 28 top / JullyFotos/Shutterstock for pages 12 bottom and 30 top / Xavier MARCHANT/Shutterstock for page 14 middle / Asian Images/Shutterstock for page 16 bottom / simongurney/© iStock for page 18 middle / Granger Historical Picture Archive/Alamy for page 22 middle / Victor de Schwanberg/ Alamy for page 24 middle / Bill Florence/Shutterstock for page 26 bottom / kwanchaichaiudom/ © iStock for pages 32 middle and 58 middle / Africa Studio/Shutterstock for pages 34 middle and 54 middle / Veran36/Shutterstock for page 36 middle / Antonio Jorge Nunes/Shutterstock for page 38 top / Monkey Business Images/Shutterstock for page 40 bottom / happyfoto/© iStock for page 46 middle / BIGANDT.COM/Shutterstock for page 48 bottom / bogdanhoria/© iStock for page 50 middle / Martyn Goddard/Alamy for page 60 bottom

CONTENTS

INTRODUCTION

Who was William Golding?   4
Plot summary   5

PLOT AND STRUCTURE

Chapters One and Two   6
Chapters Three and Four   8
Chapters Five and Six   10
Chapters Seven and Eight   12
Chapters Nine and Ten   14
Chapters Eleven and Twelve   16
Form and structure   18
Quick revision   20

SETTING AND CONTEXT

The shadow of war   22
Education and adventure   24
The island   26
Quick revision   27

CHARACTERS

Ralph   28
Jack   30
Piggy   32
Simon   34
Roger   36
Sam and Eric   38
The littluns   40
Quick revision   42

THEMES

Good and evil   44
Civilisation and savagery   46
Power and leadership   48
Fear and the beast   50
Friendship   52
Nature and religion   54
Quick revision   56

LANGUAGE

Voice and dialogue   58
Writer's effects   60

EXAM PRACTICE

Understanding the exam   62
Character questions   64
Planning your character response   66
Grade 5 annotated answer   68
Grade 7+ annotated answer   70
Theme questions   72
Planning your theme response   74
Grade 5 annotated answer   76
Grade 7+ annotated answer   78
Practice questions   80

GLOSSARY   81

ANSWERS   82

Three key things about William Golding

1. Golding was a schoolmaster's son and eventually worked as a **schoolmaster** himself, after spending time as an **actor**, **producer** and **writer**.

2. He served in the **Royal Navy** during the Second World War.

3. Golding received the **Nobel Prize** for Literature in 1983 for his novels.

What experiences did Golding have in his life?

- He studied Natural Sciences before changing to English at Brasenose College, Oxford.
- As a teacher, he understood very well how hierarchies among pupils work in schools.
- He was disgusted by people's behaviour on both sides during the war.

Why did he write *Lord of the Flies*?

- Golding was left feeling extremely pessimistic after the Second World War.
- He was angered by his countrymen's relief at being (as they thought) better than the Nazis. He believed strongly that there was the potential for evil in everyone. The war had shown him that being British did not necessarily make a person 'good'.
- He used his teacher's knowledge of how schoolboys think and act, along with his belief that anyone could 'turn bad', to inform his writing.

How important has *Lord of the Flies* been?

- *Lord of the Flies* was published in 1954 with some success, and was soon recognised as an important literary novel.
- Golding was able to leave teaching and write full time in 1961, by which time he had published three further novels.
- There are two film versions of *Lord of the Flies* and it has also been adapted for theatre. It has been studied in schools in the UK and other English-speaking countries continuously since the late 1950s.

Chapters One and Two

- Boys being evacuated in a war find themselves marooned on an island after their plane crashes.
- They elect Ralph chief and he puts Jack in charge of hunting.
- The younger boys express fears of a 'snake-thing' on the island.
- A fire is lit and gets out of control.

Chapters Three and Four

- Ralph fails to get shelters built – he does not have enough help.
- Jack, increasingly obsessed with hunting, paints his face.
- The fire burns out due to Jack's neglect and they miss a potential rescuer.
- The hunters catch a pig.

Chapters Five and Six

- The boys have a meeting and Ralph tries to re-establish rules.
- The boys discuss the 'beast' again.
- Sam and Eric mistake a dead parachutist for the beast.
- Jack leads a hunt for the beast.

Chapters Seven and Eight

- Robert is hurt in a game celebrating the hunt.
- Ralph, Jack and Roger see the parachutist and run away scared.
- The hunters kill a pig and put its head on a stick.
- The pig's head seems to speak to Simon, telling him it's the 'Lord of the Flies'.

Chapters Nine to Twelve

- Simon is killed when he is mistaken for the beast in a frenzied dance.
- Jack sets up a separate camp and attacks Ralph's camp at night, stealing Piggy's glasses.
- Roger kills Piggy up at Castle Rock by levering a rock over a cliff onto him.
- Jack's group sets the island on fire, which is seen by a passing ship and the boys are rescued.

Three key things about Chapters One and Two

1. The **island** setting is introduced: it is a place of **contrasts** with incredible **beauty** and the **threat of danger**.
2. We meet the **main characters**, boys who have survived a plane crash: **Ralph**, who is elected **chief**; **Piggy**, who **struggles** to keep up physically; and **Jack** who **bullies** Piggy immediately.
3. The idea of **order** and potential **conflict** is established as important, with the boys deciding who should be in charge and discussing **rules**.

What happens in Chapter One?

- Various boys find themselves marooned on a desert island. They assemble throughout the chapter.
- Ralph and Piggy find a conch shell, which they use to call others.
- A group of choirboys, led by Jack, marches along the beach, looking like **'something dark'**.
- Simon, one of the choirboys, faints.
- Ralph reveals Piggy's nickname to the other boys.
- The boys vote Ralph to be their chief, to Jack's disappointment. Ralph offers for Jack to lead a smaller group of hunters.
- Ralph, Jack and Simon go exploring. Jack almost kills a piglet.

What happens in Chapter Two?

- The explorers return to tell the others that there are no other people on the island.
- The boys agree that they need rules to keep themselves safe until they are rescued.
- The littluns (short for 'little ones' – the younger boys) report being afraid of a **'beastie'** on the island.
- Ralph suggests lighting a signal fire to attract rescuers. They light a fire on the mountain top using Piggy's glasses, but the fire gets out of control.
- Piggy realises that the boy with the mulberry-coloured birthmark is missing after the fire.

Five key quotations

1. Ralph's appearance and nature: 'a mildness about his mouth and eyes that proclaimed no devil' (Chapter One)
2. The island setting: 'a bird, a vision of red and yellow, flashed upwards with a witch-like cry' (Chapter One)
3. Jack introduces himself: 'I'm chapter chorister and head boy. I can sing C sharp.' (Chapter One)
4. Piggy reports what the beast is like: 'A snake-thing. Ever so big. He saw it.' (Chapter Two)
5. Piggy plays the adult: 'Like kids!' he said scornfully. 'Acting like a crowd of kids!' (Chapter Two)

Note it!

Notice how Piggy's glasses are used to light the fire, **symbolising** both Piggy's clear-sightedness and human ingenuity. Note, too, that Jack **'snatched'** them from Piggy, rather than asking for them.

Exam focus

How can I write about contrasts? AO2

You can use Chapter One to write about contrasts in the setting.

> Golding creates a setting which is full of contrasts. On the first page, Ralph's progress is halted when 'a bird, a vision of red and yellow, flashed upwards with a witch-like cry'. This shows both the startling and exotic beauty of the island, and its potential threat to the boys. The adjective 'witch-like' could be seen as an example of foreshadowing, warning the reader of danger to come.

Topic sentence makes overall point

Embedded quotation to illustrate

Explanation of contrast illustrated by quotation

Linguistic terminology 'zooms in' for analysis

Literary terminology used to analyse effect

Now you try!

Finish this paragraph about how Piggy is introduced. Use one of the quotations from the list.

The opening chapters introduce the idea of conflict through the presentation of Piggy, who is lecturing the other ....

Three key things about Chapters Three and Four

1. **Savagery** on the island develops rapidly, through the hunting party's face-painting, **failures in rules** and routines and the **increasing cruelty** to the littluns and Piggy.

2. **Ralph's** concern for **order** and **civilisation** is made clearer with his focus on building shelters and his anger about the fire being allowed to go out.

3. Secondary characters such as Roger and Simon are developed in more detail as we begin to see **Roger's cruelty** and **Simon's natural helpfulness**.

What happens in Chapter Three?

- The chapter opens with Jack on a solo hunt, which is unsuccessful.
- Ralph is frustrated that he is not getting enough help with building shelters – although everyone agrees to work, they wander off after five minutes. He sees Jack's hunting as a fun activity, but one which does not help their safety on the island or their rescue.
- Jack, Simon and Ralph mention the beast again as another reason shelters are needed.
- Simon goes into the forest alone, after helping littluns reach high-up fruit.

What happens in Chapter Four?

- The littluns play in the sand. Maurice and Roger spoil their game and Roger throws stones around Henry, but does not quite dare to throw them at him directly.

- Jack and the hunters paint their faces to help them sneak up on the pigs.
- Simon, Piggy and Ralph see a ship go by, but the hunters have forgotten to keep the signal fire alight.
- The hunters return chanting triumphantly with their first dead pig but Ralph and Piggy's response is to shout at them for letting the fire go out.
- Jack reacts angrily and smashes a lens in Piggy's glasses. He apologises about the fire.

Five key quotations

1. Jack's obsession with hunting: 'He tried to convey the compulsion to track down and kill that was swallowing him up.' (Chapter Three)
2. Ralph on Simon's uniqueness: 'He's queer. He's funny.' (Chapter Three)
3. Structures of civilisation: 'Round the squatting child was the protection of parents and school and policemen and the law.' (Chapter Four)
4. Ralph's anger: he 'reached inside himself for the worst word he knew. "They let the bloody fire out."' (Chapter Four)
5. Signs of savagery: 'Kill the pig. Cut her throat. Spill her blood.' (Chapter Four)

Note it!

Notice how Piggy is not taken seriously in these chapters. He has an idea to make sundials, showing his link to science and knowledge, but Ralph mocks him. Later, when the hunters return with meat, Piggy is the one they deliberately and explicitly leave out.

Exam focus

How can I write about the balance of civilisation and savagery? AO1

You can use these chapters to write about how civilisation begins to descend into savagery.

In Chapter Four, Roger's natural cruelty leads him to destroy the littluns' games in the sand, yet the structures of civilisation still hold, preventing him from hurting Henry. Golding shows that 'Round the squatting child was the protection of parents and school and policemen and the law.' This symbolic 'protection' demonstrates how the boys have initially brought civilised ideas with them to the island, operating as though these institutions still exist around them.

Clear comment on character

Concise reference to theme, linking to question

Reference to literary technique of symbolism

Development of idea relating to theme

Now you try!

Finish this paragraph about the move away from civilisation. Use another of the quotations from the list.

Golding portrays the breaking down of civilisation into savagery soon after the boys' arrival on the island. This can be seen in Chapter Three when Jack ....

PLOT AND STRUCTURE Chapters Five and Six

Three key things about Chapters Five and Six

1. Ralph's **leadership skills** are emphasised. It is clear that he deserves to be chief, but also that the boys are not following his lead.
2. The **threat of the beast** becomes more important and begins to **divide** the boys.
3. The **island landscape** is developed in more detail.

What happens in Chapter Five?

- Ralph prepares for and holds an assembly to **'put things straight'**. He tries to re-establish rules like cleanliness and organisation and the boys discuss the beast.
- Jack, Piggy, and Ralph agree there is no beast on the island.
- Simon gets philosophical in talking about the beast: **'maybe it's only us.'**
- A littlun, Percival, tries to talk and becomes stuck on reciting his name, address and phone number, which he can no longer fully remember.
- Ralph, Piggy and Simon wish things were as simple and organised as in the grown-up world. Ralph asks for a sign from the outside world.

What happens in Chapter Six?

- A dead parachutist is blown onto the mountain-top.
- Sam and Eric are guarding the signal fire and mistake the parachutist for the beast when they relight the fire.
- An assembly is called about the beast and order begins to break down. Jack states that some have more right to speak than others, regardless of the conch, but Ralph holds power.
- Jack, Ralph and Simon lead a hunt for the beast while Piggy stays behind to look after the littluns.
- Ralph goes ahead in the hunt and the boys find a good place for a fort. Once again, Ralph has to remind the others of practicalities as they carry on in their quest.

Five key quotations

1. Jack's challenge to Ralph: 'Who are you, anyway? Sitting there – telling people what to do. You can't hunt. You can't sing—' (Chapter Five)

2. The island as dangerous: 'Then the sleeping leviathan breathed out – the waters rose, the weed streamed, and the water boiled over the table rock with a roar.' (Chapter Six)

3. Fear of the beast: 'Soon the darkness was full of claws, full of the awful unknown and menace.' (Chapter Five)

4. Breakdown in order: '... we don't need the conch any more. We know who ought to say things.' (Jack, Chapter Six)

5. Ralph's leadership: 'I'm chief. We've got to make certain.' (Chapter Six)

Note it!

When the boys reach the end of the island and see what a good place for a fort it is, most of them are overtaken by savagery. Their initial desire is to be destructive, rolling rocks down the mountainside.

Exam focus

How can I write about Ralph and Jack's relationship? AO1 AO2

You can use Chapters Five and Six to explore the widening gap between Ralph and Jack.

> Order begins to break down in the novel as Ralph and Jack's relationship becomes more strained. By the middle of the novel, Jack is challenging Ralph's power directly, asking 'Who are you, anyway? Sitting there – telling people what to do.' He goes on to hint that he feels he should be leader: 'You can't hunt. You can't sing.' These verbs, 'hunt' and 'sing', emphasise physical skills that he has and that Ralph lacks.

Topic sentence links theme with characters' relationship

Quotation is embedded and explained

Point is developed

Language analysis develops ideas further

Now you try!

Finish this further paragraph about the conflict between Ralph and Jack. Use one of the quotations from the list.

Jack and Ralph's growing conflict can also be seen through Golding's exploration of the theme of order. It is presented through Jack's outburst ....

Three key things about Chapters Seven and Eight

1. The boys' **violence increases** with physical harm to Robert through the hunting game, foreshadowing Simon's death.

2. The boys **separate** into two groups, the conch group maintaining **routines for rescue** and Jack's group emphasising **physical pleasure** in a self-indulgent way.

3. **Simon**'s vision of the Lord of the Flies develops his **outsider** status and the **beast** as symbol.

What happens in Chapter Seven?

- The chapter opens with Ralph's thoughts about the boys' physical state.
- Simon tells Ralph he'll get home, which Ralph dismisses as Simon being **'batty'**.
- After a boar they chase escapes, the boys play at hunting and turn on Robert, who gets hurt.
- Ralph wants to break off the beast hunt once it gets dark, but Jack taunts him for being scared.
- Ralph, Jack and Roger go up the mountain to look for the beast. Faced with the parachutist in the moonlight, they flee.

What happens in Chapter Eight?

- Ralph, Jack and Roger report back. Jack says his hunters could kill the beast, but Ralph insults them by saying they couldn't.
- Jack calls a meeting. He says Ralph is not fit to be chief and tries to lead a mutiny. Jack leaves, inviting the others to hunt with him.
- The conch group build a fire near the platform, at Piggy's suggestion, and realise that many boys have gradually joined Jack.
- The hunters kill a sow who had piglets and make an offering to the beast of her head on a stick.
- Jack and some of his hunters steal fire from the conch group. Jack invites other boys to join him to feast.
- Simon enters the forest alone. In a trance, he has a conversation with the pig's head (labelled the Lord of the Flies).

Five key quotations

1. Simon's message of hope to Ralph: 'You'll get back to where you came from.' (Chapter Seven)

2. Violent emotions stirred up by the hunting game: 'The desire to squeeze and hurt was over-mastering.' (Chapter Seven)

3. Piggy's idea: 'Only Piggy could have the intellectual daring to suggest moving the fire from the mountain.' (Chapter Eight)

4. Jack's primitivism: 'When we kill we'll leave some of the kill for it. Then it won't bother us, maybe.' (Chapter Eight)

5. Simon hears the beast speak from the pig's head: 'Fancy thinking the Beast was something you could hunt and kill!... You knew, didn't you? I'm part of you?' (Chapter Eight)

Note it!

Golding manipulates the novel's pace as the boys hunt and become more savage. As their fear increases, the average sentence length decreases. The boys' savagery is associated with a breakdown in their language, e.g. their tribalistic chants in the hunt.

Exam focus

How can I write about the beast? AO1 AO2

You can write about how Golding uses the beast in Jack's character development.

Golding uses the concept of the beast to develop aspects of character. In Jack's case, having earlier denied the beast, his attitude here shows his shift into savagery by leaving offerings as though the beast were a primitive god: 'When we kill, we'll leave some of the kill for it. Then it won't bother us, maybe.' This ritualistic behaviour, along with simple sentence structure, shows how Jack's character is descending into primitive ways of thinking.

- Clear topic sentence
- Strong statement of key theme
- Explanation linking quotation to theme
- Brief comment on language
- Restated theme phrased effectively

Now you try!

Finish this paragraph about a different character. Use one of the quotations from the list.

Golding also uses the idea of the beast to show how Simon's character develops. When he communicates with ....

Three key things about Chapters Nine and Ten

1. The different values of the two groups are underlined: pleasure and **savagery** for Jack's tribe, preparation and **equality** for Ralph's group.

2. The **savagery** becomes lethal with Simon's death, which causes different reactions: Ralph states it was **'murder'**, but Piggy, the clearest thinker, describes it as an **'accident'**. Jack's tribe only sees Simon as the **beast**.

3. **Simon's presentation** as a Christ-like figure is clearest when he rushes from the mountain to share the truth like a prophet and is **killed**. The shining sea-creatures that surround his body appear like a **halo**.

What happens in Chapter Nine?

- Simon wakes and discovers the dead parachutist. He realises the truth and decides to tell the others.

- Ralph and Piggy walk near Jack's group and Jack orders them to be given some meat.

- Jack demands to know who will join his **'tribe'** and Jack and Ralph argue about the conch's significance.

- During a ritualistic dance, Simon comes out of the forest into the chanting circle. He is mistaken for the beast, and killed.

- The storm arrives in full force after Simon's death. It helps blow the parachutist's body down off the mountainside. It is washed out to sea with Simon's body.

What happens in Chapter Ten?

- Ralph's group discuss Simon's death. They all agree they were very tired and were not really part of it.

- Jack's tribe sets up camp at the end of the island. His clear rules include beatings as punishments. Roger is happy to have a **'proper chief'**.

- With too little wood to keep a fire burning all the time, Ralph's group decide to let it go out at night. Ralph appears confused and has muddled dreams about home.

- Jack leads a night-time raid on Ralph's camp and steals Piggy's glasses.

Five key quotations

1. Loss of order: 'the conch doesn't count at this end of the island—' (Jack to Ralph, Chapter Nine)

2. The death of Simon: 'There were no words, and no movements but the tearing of teeth and claws.' (Chapter Nine)

3. Responsibility for Simon's death: 'Don't you understand, Piggy? The things we did—' (Ralph, Chapter Ten)

4. Unity in Ralph's group: 'Memory of the dance that none of them had attended shook all four boys convulsively.' (Chapter Ten)

5. Jack's leadership: 'He was a chief now in truth; and he made stabbing motions with his spear.' (Chapter Ten)

Note it!

Chapter Ten is entitled 'The Shell and the Glasses', both important **symbols** in the novel. When Jack raids Ralph's camp, Piggy's instinct is to protect the conch, because to him it is a symbol of democracy. To Jack, however, it is worthless, while the glasses can create fire.

Exam focus

How can I write about context?

You can use these chapters to explore how the two groups relate to the novel's historical context.

Golding contrasts Ralph and Jack as representing democracy and dictatorship, in the Cold War context of the 1950s. Ralph's leadership style is collaborative and democratic, which Golding shows as encouraging unity among the boys in his group: 'Memory of the dance that none of them had attended shook all four boys convulsively.' This emphasis on shared experience with 'none' and 'all' shows their connection to one another, developed through Ralph's leadership.

> Topic sentence makes point clear
>
> Explicit link to context
>
> Clear sense of author
>
> Focus on specific word choices and effect

Now you try!

Finish this paragraph about context. Use one of the quotations from the list.

A function of Jack's tribe is to represent dictatorships. The idea of the inequality in his camp is explored when he tells Ralph ....

Three key things about Chapters Eleven and Twelve

1. **Ralph** and **Piggy** cling to the last remnants of **order**: they want to approach Jack looking clean and tidy with the conch.
2. **Piggy**'s death, holding the **conch**, marks the **end** of order and civilisation.
3. **Jack**'s determination to kill **Ralph** results in the **destruction** of the island's natural resources, showing his complete **loss of reason**.

What happens in Chapter Eleven?

- Ralph's group cannot light a fire, so resolve to confront Jack and demand Piggy's glasses back.
- Ralph and Samneric go to Castle Rock with Piggy, where guards have been told not to allow them entry. Jack returns from hunting; he and Ralph fight.
- Piggy shouts, trying to make Jack's tribe see sense and act responsibly. Roger levers a huge rock onto Piggy and kills him, smashing the conch.
- Jack throws a spear at Ralph, wounding him, and Ralph runs off into the forest.
- Jack and Roger attack Samneric for not joining the tribe.

What happens in Chapter Twelve?

- Ralph hides in the forest until evening, seeing the pig's skull in the clearing. Watching Castle Rock, and thinking about his options, he is sad to recognise Samneric on watch.
- Ralph learns from Samneric that they were forced to join the tribe, that Jack will hunt Ralph the next day and that Roger has **'sharpened a stick at both ends'**.
- The hunt begins next morning; boys chase Ralph through the forest, rolling rocks down the mountainside at him.
- Jack sets part of the forest on fire to smoke Ralph out. The smoke is seen by a passing ship.
- Ralph collapses on the beach and looks up to see a naval officer, who ironically assumes the boys have been playing at war.

Five key quotations

1. Jack's poor priorities: 'Do you remember how he went hunting and the fire went out and a ship passed by?' (Ralph, Chapter Eleven)

2. Piggy clings to civilisation: 'You let me carry the conch, Ralph. I'll show him the one thing he hasn't got.' (Chapter Eleven)

3. Jack's loss of reason: 'The fire must be almost at the fruit trees – what would they eat tomorrow.' (Ralph, Chapter Twelve)

4. Naval officer's assumptions about boys' adventure: 'I know. Jolly good show. Like the Coral Island.' (Chapter Twelve)

5. Human nature: 'Ralph wept for the end of innocence, the darkness of man's heart, and the fall through the air of the true, wise friend called Piggy.' (Chapter Twelve)

Note it!

Ralph's inability to understand Samneric's warning that **'Roger has sharpened a stick at both ends'** shows how detached from the hunters' new reality he is. The reader has observed both groups and understands that this means he will be hunted like a pig, but the meaning is unclear to Ralph.

Exam focus

How can I write about irony? AO2

You can use the novel's ending to write about irony.

> Golding uses heavy irony at the end of the novel, to emphasise the difference between the naval officer's view and reality. The officer assumes that the boys are innocent and playful, calling it a Jolly good show. Like the Coral Island.' This reference to a children's adventure book, with its idealised fantasy of boys cooperating on a desert island is the opposite of the violence that Ralph is running from.

Topic sentence makes point clear

Quotation is embedded effectively into ideas

Explanation of what Coral Island represents

Clear analysis of the irony

Now you try!

Finish this paragraph about symbolism in the novel. Use one of the quotations from the list.

The novel's closing chapters make use of the symbolism that threads through the book. Golding reintroduces the symbol of the signal fire to ....

Three key things about form and structure

1. The form relates to the **adventure genre**. It subverts this **genre**, as usually these tales are upbeat, celebrating survival skills in overcoming obstacles.

2. The **novel's structure** is linear or **chronological** but the precise passage of time is unclear, probably due to the boys' loss of ability to mark time.

3. The novel is **allegorical**: characters, objects and plot events have **symbolic** meanings and may be interpreted in different ways.

How does Golding use the adventure novel form?

- Boys are marooned on a desert island, where they must look after themselves without adults.

- Some of the novel's most exciting passages are derived from hunting, clearly enjoyed by many of the boys.

- Initially, the boys are excited to be on an island, and they are keen to explore. They see the island as inherently good.

In what ways does the novel follow a three-act structure?

- **Setup**: The characters explore and learn about their surroundings and they develop in response to their new setting.

- **Confrontation**: Jack breaks away from the other boys and this stage ends with Simon's conversation with the pig's head. Piggy's death is the climax.

- **Climax and resolution**: This is approached through the boys' increasing violence and the murders of Simon and Piggy. They intend to also kill Ralph, but this is prevented by the arrival of the naval officer – only external intervention can prevent full tragedy.

What allegorical readings of the novel are possible?

- Characters represent ideas, e.g.: Piggy – logic; Ralph – order; Jack – savagery.

- Political allegory: Ralph represents democracy and Jack symbolises dictatorship.

Five key quotations

1. Time: 'He would like to have a pair of scissors and cut this hair – he flung the mass back – cut this filthy hair right back to half an inch.' (Ralph, Chapter Seven)

2. Adventure: 'this is a good island. We – Jack, Simon and me – we climbed the mountain. It's wizard. There's food and drink, ...' (Ralph, Chapter Two)

3. Exploring the other end of the island: 'This would make a wizard fort.' (Chapter Six)

4. Survival and the fire: 'Ralph's told you often enough,' said Piggy moodily. 'How else are we going to be rescued?' (Chapter Ten)

5. Novel's climax: 'Piggy's arms and legs twitched a bit, like a pig's after it has been killed.' (Chapter Eleven)

Note it!

Golding subverts the adventure novel form to illustrate his view that everyone has both good and evil within. This subversion allows him to show the boys introducing evil to the island, rather than dealing only with difficulties that already existed there.

Exam focus

How can I write about allegory? AO2

You can use the presentation of Piggy as logical and reasoned, to write about allegory.

Using allegory makes the novel's themes sharper and more obvious, as they are carried in multiple ways in the text.	Clear statement of the point
Piggy's comments are often like an adult's,	Link made to character
chastising the other boys: 'Ralph's told you often enough,' said Piggy moodily. 'How else are we going to be rescued?',	Relevance of quotation explained
making his role as representing logic and reason clear. This is further underscored by his association with the symbol of the glasses.	Point developed in more detail

Now you try!

Finish this paragraph linking theme to form and structure in the novel. Use one of the quotations from the list.

Golding uses the novel's structure to clearly show the breakdown of order on the island. This is clear when the climax ....

1. Look at this ideas map representing Chapters One and Two. Is there anything else you can add?

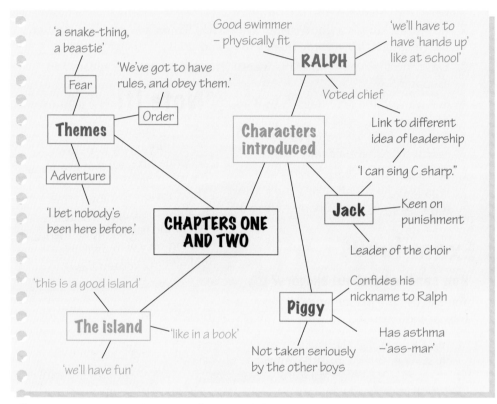

2. Create your own ideas map for one of the other sections.

Quick quiz

Answer these quick questions about the novel's plot and structure.

1. Who are the first two boys we encounter in the book?
2. Who knows how to blow the conch?
3. How does the first death on the island happen?
4. Why is Ralph angry with Jack after the first hunt?
5. What are the younger boys scared of on the island?
6. What does Simon suggest is the thing they are really scared of?

7. What genre of novel is *Lord of the Flies* based upon?
8. Who throws stones around Henry, but doesn't dare aim them at him?
9. Name three things that Ralph remembers about home at any point in the novel.
10. What do the hunters leave out as an offering?
11. What is the 'Lord of the Flies'?
12. What do Samneric see and get frightened by?
13. How does Simon get killed?
14. Who looks after the littluns when others go hunting for the beast?
15. Why do Samneric join Jack's tribe?
16. What event causes the 'confrontation' stage in the novel?
17. Who steals Piggy's glasses?
18. What gets broken when Piggy is killed?
19. How does Ralph learn that he is to be hunted?
20. How does the naval officer come to realise there are people on the island?

Power paragraphs

Write **a paragraph** in response to **each of these questions**. For each, try to use **one quotation** you have learned from this section.

1. In what ways does Golding show how Ralph and Piggy are very different in the opening chapters?
2. Why does Golding choose to include the incident where Roger throws stones around Henry, but not at him?

Exam practice

Re-read the section in Chapter Eight where Jack calls an assembly (pages 137–140).

Why is this moment significant in the text as a whole? Write **two paragraphs** explaining your ideas. You could comment on:

- Jack's relationship with Ralph
- the theme of fear.

SETTING AND CONTEXT The shadow of war

Five key things about the shadow of war

1. The **Second World War** still had a huge effect in Britain well **into the 1950s**.
2. Many people had had **personal experience of fighting** which had affected them deeply. Others had lost friends and family.
3. The war left many **Britons** feeling pleased they had been on the **'right' side**. Golding did not feel this, having seen **cruelty from some British forces**.
4. The **Cold War** followed the Second World War, lasting until about **1989–1991**.
5. The threat from **atomic weapons** caused paranoia and **tension**.

What was the Cold War?

- This was an indirect battle between the Eastern Bloc, led by the USSR (Soviet Russia) and the West, led by the USA. It was 'cold' because there was no direct fighting.
- The Cold War was ideological, i.e. based on opposing ideas and beliefs.
- The USSR was run under totalitarian communist principles, while the USA represented the principles of capitalist democracy.
- Both sides involved themselves in conflicts in other parts of the world to gain more power (e.g. their involvement in the Korean War 1950–3) but they did not fight each other directly.

BOMB TESTS

How did the Cold War affect people's lives?

- The Cold War brought continual tension between global superpowers, so there was a constant threat of possible war.
- In the West (i.e. the USA and its allies), communism became the new enemy.
- The tensions encouraged black and white thinking (i.e. simplistic views that things can only be, for example, good or bad, with no 'grey areas').

What was the atom bomb?

- It was a nuclear-type weapon, like the one used on Hiroshima in 1944.
- There were school drills in what to do if the 'four-minute warning' sounded to alert of impending nuclear strike.

Three key quotations

1. **Britishness:** 'I should have thought that a pack of British boys ... would have been able to put up a better show than that—' (naval officer, Chapter Twelve)

2. **Effects of war:** 'They're all dead.' (Piggy, Chapter One)

3. **Two opposing sides on the island:** 'We hunt and feast and have fun. If you want to join my tribe come and see us.' (Jack, Chapter Eight)

Note it!

The naval officer assumes the boys have been playing at war when he arrives. Golding uses this attitude to contrast a typical view of childhood innocence with how far the boys have strayed from civilisation.

Exam focus

How do I link context to the novel? AO3

The Cold War context can be used to discuss central ideas connected to the key main characters.

Golding creates an increasingly tense atmosphere in the novel, as relations between Ralph and Jack, representatives of democracy and totalitarianism, become more and more difficult. The boys begin as friends, just as the two Cold War sides allied against Hitler, but gradually Ralph's insistence on the signal fire and conch and Jack's desire to 'hunt and feast' above all else shows their separate values.

Characters clearly linked to context

Connection made between context and structure

Quotation integrated effectively

Clear explanation

Now you try!

Finish this paragraph about the novel's context. Use one of the quotations from the list.

Views of Western and specifically British identity in the Cold War context are explored by Golding through the novel. For example, when the naval officer rescues the boys ....

SETTING AND CONTEXT Education and adventure

Five key things about education and adventure

1. All the key characters are **schoolboys**, probably from public schools.
2. Golding's personal experience as a **teacher** makes his schoolboys **realistic**.
3. In the 1950s, when the book was set, children had much more **freedom** to **explore** and play unsupervised than today's children. They were also viewed as more **innocent** and unworldly.
4. **Exploration** and discovery of tropical islands would seem like a grand **adventure** in 1954, when foreign travel was far less common than today.
5. There was great interest in **science**, **space travel** and **exploration** at this time.

What was the UK school system like in 1954?

- Schools were either public (paid for by parents) or state (funded by taxes). Some public-school places were given as scholarships to poorer children.

- Children were divided at age 11 into grammar (academic) or secondary modern (vocational) schools.
- Public and grammar schools created a highly-structured environment based on established tradition and strict rules.

What is the adventure genre?

- The adventure genre presents heroic protagonists overcoming dangerous obstacles, often in an unfamiliar environment. It was popular in the 1950s.
- *The Coral Island*, mentioned twice in *Lord of the Flies*, is a typical example of an adventure novel. In it, Ralph, Jack (no coincidence) and Peterkin work together against vicious native inhabitants and dangerous animals.
- Golding subverts the genre by making the boys themselves the evil element.

Why did Golding use schoolboys as his main characters?

- He wanted to show that evil was present even in an innocent child.
- The fact that it is the head choirboy with a pure singing voice who leads the savage tribe is significant.
- Golding also shows the boys initially trying to implement routines and rules **'like at school'**, but the shift from order to chaos is inevitable.

Three key quotations

1. Schoolboy skills: 'I can sing C sharp.' (Jack, Chapter One)
2. Parallel with adventure stories: 'It's like in a book.'... 'Treasure Island—' 'Swallows and Amazons—' 'Coral Island—' (Ralph, unnamed replies, Chapter Two)
3. School discipline: 'Remember old Waxy at school?' 'Boy—you-are-driving-me-slowly-insane!" (Eric, Sam, Chapter Six)

Note it!

The boys could also seek to discover their environment on the island properly, and try to continue their education by learning more about the island and its wildlife. Arguably, the fact that they do not is one reason **'things break up'**. Ralph tries to understand this after the groups split.

Exam focus

How can I write about literary context? AO3

The context of adventure novels can be used to write about the themes of the novel.

> Golding makes an explicit link to adventure novels at the start of the novel, with boys excitedly shouting out the names 'Treasure Island–', 'Swallows and Amazons–', 'Coral Island–', while Ralph is trying to explain about the island. The book titles are used to show the boys' enthusiasm for the adventure that they believe lies before them. This shows how the novel starts symbolically in a place of order and good.

Clearly stated topic sentence

Quotation is well contextualised

Effect of contextual information explained

Subtle indication that the boys are wrong

Connection made to novel's themes

Now you try!

Finish this paragraph referring to the context of education in the novel. Use one of the quotations above.

The context of the boys' education is used by Golding to support the novel's themes. This is seen when Jack argues ....

Five key things about the island

1. The novel is **entirely set** on the island, where the boys are trapped and **isolated** from society.
2. The boys gradually explore the island, revealing different types of **landscape**.
3. Initially, Ralph describes the island as a **'good'** island and it is claimed as **'our island'** (Chapter Two). It can be seen as a **symbol** of **paradise** or Garden of Eden, which is then spoiled by the boys.
4. It is an uninhabited island with edible, non-threatening animals – except for the **perceived threat** of the beast.
5. The island, as presented by Golding, is **neither wholly good nor bad**. The **forces of nature** are clearly presented as both at different times.

Why is the platform significant in the novel?

- The platform is where meetings are held, and the conch group remain near it once Jack's group breaks off.
- Its importance is shown through extended description in Chapter One.
- The platform, with its square shape and solidity, represents order.

How is the pool important to the novel?

- The pool is where Ralph shows Piggy how well he swims.
- The boys use it for leisure – swimming and diving.
- One of Ralph's earliest complaints is of the boys not keeping the pool clean, showing how civilisation starts to break down.

How is Castle Rock important to the novel?

- Castle Rock is associated with fun from the first time it is discovered – Ralph has difficulty getting the others to concentrate on why they went there.
- Jack's tribe colonises it and it becomes his fortress. It becomes associated with violence and giving in to pleasure.

In what ways are the forest and the mountain top significant?

- The forest is used for hunting and is dark and mysterious. It is also where the pig's head is left as an offering and later speaks to Simon.
- The mountain top is important initially for practicalities: checking the island layout and lighting the signal fire. Later, in the boys' fearful minds, it becomes overtaken by the beast (in fact, parachutist).

Quick quiz

1. Who was involved in the Cold War?
2. Name two children's 'adventure' books.
3. Where do the boys swim?
4. What kind of school did you go to in the 1950s if you were academic?
5. What is an atom bomb?
6. How did the Cold War affect people's thinking?
7. Where do the conch group end up?
8. Why did Golding not feel glad to be British after the war?
9. Where does most of the hunting in the novel take place?
10. What aspects of school routine are most relevant to the novel?

Power paragraphs

Choose one key setting or context related to the novel. Write **two paragraphs** explaining how Golding makes use of this setting or context in relation to either a) theme or b) character.

Five key things about Ralph

1. Golding focuses our attention on **Ralph** at the **start of the novel** as he is the first boy we 'see'. This positions him as the protagonist.
2. **Ralph** is elected **chief** (because of his association with the **conch**).
3. He represents **democracy**, **order**, **citizenship** and **moral goodness**.
4. He tries to keep the boys **focused** on what they **need to do** to be **rescued**.
5. He is the one to speak to the **naval officer** at the end.

What do we learn about Ralph at the beginning of the novel?

- Ralph is fair-haired, physically fit and a good swimmer.
- He is playful: standing on his head out of joy and excitement.
- He is confident, taking it for granted that they will be rescued.
- He is diplomatic – when he reveals Piggy's nickname to the other boys, he placates him by arguing that it is **'Better … than Fatty'**.
- He is fair-minded, as he suggests Jack being in charge of the choirboys when he is disappointed at not being chief.

How does Ralph develop?

- **Chapter Four**: Ralph takes his leadership role seriously, being angry about the signal fire going out.
- **Chapter Five**: He plans for a meeting and starts to show more respect for Piggy as a thinker.
- **Chapter Nine**: He joins in the game that hurts Robert (Chapter Seven) and the dance that kills Simon.
- **Chapter Ten**: He is the only boy to acknowledge, even for a moment, that they killed Simon.
- **Chapter Twelve**: Having used up all his resources, he appears as uncivilised as the other boys, despite not having given in to savagery in the same way. He ends the novel in a fit of **'grief'**, which spreads to the littluns but not the remaining older boys.

Five key quotations

1. Initial description of Ralph: 'there was a mildness about his mouth and eyes that proclaimed no devil' (Chapter One)
2. Ralph (to Jack): 'Don't you want to be rescued? All you can talk about is pig, pig, pig!' (Chapter Three)
3. Ralph's thoughts on leadership: 'The trouble was, if you were a chief you had to think, you had to be wise.' (Chapter Five)
4. Ralph (to the conch group): 'I'd like to put on war-paint and be a savage. But we must keep the fire burning.' (Chapter Eight)
5. Description of Ralph at the end: 'with filthy body, matted hair, and unwiped nose, Ralph wept ... ' (Chapter Twelve)

Note it!

Note that, as savagery takes over the boys, Ralph has moments where he forgets why they need to keep the fire burning and Piggy has to remind him.

Exam focus

How can I write about Ralph at the start of the novel? AO1

You can comment on how Golding presents Ralph as good and sensible.

At the start of the novel, Golding immediately presents Ralph as kind and moral. In describing Ralph, Golding clearly uses terms aligning him with good rather than evil: 'mildness that proclaimed no devil'. His association with goodness in the theme of good and evil is also indicated by the use of the noun 'mildness', which suggests he is a kind and gentle boy.

Topic sentence refers to specific point in novel

Relevant quotation is linked to a theme

Explains Ralph's link to theme explicitly

Analyses, using specific reference to language

Now you try!

Finish this paragraph about Ralph's development. Use one of the quotations from the list.

Golding shows how Ralph develops as a representative of civilisation in the novel by showing how ....

Five key things about Jack

1. **Jack** believes he has more **right to be leader** than Ralph.
2. He quickly becomes **obsessed with hunting**.
3. He represents **evil**, **chaos**, **savagery** and **ideas associated with totalitarianism**.
4. He doesn't believe in the **beast**, but **uses the boys' fear** of it for his own purposes.
5. His **violence** increases until he **hunts Ralph** deliberately, **intending to kill** him.

What do we learn about Jack at the beginning of the novel?

- As well as being head boy at school, Jack was also lead chorister.
- He is tall and bony with red hair.
- The other choirboys call him by his last name, Merridew.
- He is quick to pick on Piggy, who he has just met, calling him **'Fatty'** and telling him to **'shut up'**.
- Jack is arrogant: he feels disappointment when Ralph is elected chief, but is happy to lead the choir and make them hunters.

How does Jack develop?

- **Chapter Two**: Jack likes the idea of rules because rule-breakers could be punished, but ultimately he doesn't follow the rules himself.
- **Chapter Three**: Jack is the first to feel overwhelmed in the hunt before the feeling takes over the rest of the boys.
- **Chapter Four**: Having agreed to split the choir into two teams to keep the fire burning, irresponsibly he takes the whole group hunting and lets the fire go out.
- **Chapter Eight**: When he splits the group, he leads his hunters in killing a sow with piglets, which is unwise as the piglets could have provided meat in the future.
- **Chapter Eleven**: When he leads his own tribe, he is shown as a cruel leader, punishing boys and not treating them as individuals.

Five key quotations

1. Jack's entrance: 'something dark was fumbling along ... The creature was a party of boys' (Chapter One)
2. Attitude to hunting: Jack had a 'compulsion to track down and kill that was swallowing him up.' (Chapter Three)
3. Jack on leadership: 'Who are you, anyway? Sitting there – telling people what to do. You can't hunt, you can't sing—' (Chapter Five)
4. Jack to his tribe: 'This head is for the beast. It's a gift.' (Chapter Eight)
5. To Ralph, after Piggy's death: 'See? See? That's what you'll get! I meant that! There isn't a tribe for you any more! The conch is gone—' (Chapter Eleven)

Note it!

Jack is presented negatively, as the antagonist. His hair, **'red beneath the black cap'**, is intended as a warning signal, and his behaviour is mean from the start. He is also responsible for lost rescue opportunities and poor survival choices.

Exam focus

How can I write about Jack at the start of the novel? AO1 AO2

You can comment on how Golding presents Jack in a negative way.

In the opening chapter, Golding introduces Jack and the choir with threatening imagery. The boys gathering on the beach notice 'something dark' in the distance, eventually realising that 'the darkness was not all shadow but mostly clothing. The creature was a party of boys.' This description foreshadows some kind of disaster, with the connotations of evil invoked through words like 'darkness' and 'creature'.

Topic sentence refers to specific point in novel

Relevant quotation is fluently embedded

Literary term used to explain effect

Link made to key theme

Focuses on Golding's specific language choices

Now you try!

Finish this paragraph about Jack's development. Use one of the quotations from the list.

Golding uses Jack to contribute to the novel's presentation of savagery by ....

Five key things about Piggy

1. **Piggy** is generally **not taken seriously** by the other boys, except by Ralph as the novel progresses.
2. He represents **logic**, **reason** and the **adult** way of approaching problems.
3. He lacks **personal and social skills** in presenting his good ideas to the other boys and is often a **figure of fun**.
4. He values the **conch** above all else and always remembers the **significance of the fire**.
5. He is clearly **working class** and appears to be the **most intelligent** of the boys.

What do we learn about Piggy at the beginning of the novel?

- Piggy is overweight and finds physical activity difficult.
- He has asthma (**'ass-mar'**) and wears glasses.
- He was known as 'Piggy' at school and did not like this nickname – we do not know his actual name.
- His parents are dead and he lived with his auntie.
- He speaks using non-standard grammar, showing his lower-class status.

How does Piggy develop?

- **Chapter One**: Piggy suggests they use the conch to call others and tells Ralph how to blow it.
- **Chapter One**: He tells the other boys off for abandoning shelter-building and setting a fire without enough care. This type of scolding becomes a pattern, to which Jack reacts negatively.
- **Chapter Five**: He says the idea of beasts doesn't make sense and applies rational thought to the problem of fear.
- **Chapter Ten**: Overtaken by the savagery involved in Simon's death, he cannot make sense of it, so denies the event.
- **Chapter Eleven**: He carries the conch ceremonially to Jack when asking for his glasses back, so when he is killed by a giant rock, the conch is also crushed.

Five key quotations

1. Piggy to the boys: 'How can you expect to be rescued if you don't put first things first and act proper?' (Chapter Two)

2. Piggy about Jack: 'If you're scared of someone you hate him but you can't stop thinking about him.' (Chapter Five)

3. Piggy: 'We could experiment. We could find out how to make a small hot fire and then put green branches on to make smoke.' (Chapter Eight)

4. On Simon's death: 'We was scared!' said Piggy excitedly. 'Anything might have happened. It wasn't — what you said.' (Chapter Ten)

5. About Jack at the end: 'I'm going to him with this conch in my hands.' (Chapter Eleven)

Note it!

Golding presents Piggy with irony. He is the most metaphorically clear-sighted of the boys, seeing what needs to be done and finding solutions, although literally he has the worst sight.

Exam focus

How can I write about Piggy at the start of the novel? AO1 AO2

You can comment on how Golding introduces Piggy as a difficult character to like.

From the beginning, Golding presents Piggy's lecturing tone as annoying. When the fire burns out of control, he scolds the boys, demanding, 'How can you expect to be rescued if you don't put first things first and act proper?'. His is the adult view, but his use of phrases such as 'act proper' also suggests that he believes there is one correct way to behave.

Opening sentence links character and topic

Relevant quotation is embedded effectively

Hint of what Piggy represents here

Beginnings of language analysis with sharper focus

Now you try!

Finish this paragraph about Piggy later in the novel. Use one of the quotations from the list above.

Golding shows how Piggy represents logic and is linked to the theme of civilisation in his approach to ....

Five key things about Simon

1. **Simon** is a clear **outsider** from the start, viewed as **'batty'** by the other boys.
2. He has **fits** and **faints**, communicating with the **Lord of the Flies** during one episode.
3. He can be seen as a **prophet** character and may be intended as a **Christ-like** figure.
4. He **works** alongside the older boys, e.g. exploring, hunting for the **beast**.
5. His death highlights the boys' relationship to **responsibility**: even **Piggy** cannot accept the truth, while the savage tribe describe him only as **'the beast'** or **'it'**.

What do we learn about Simon at the beginning of the novel?

- The other choristers do not treat him seriously, giggling at his fainting fits.
- He is small and skinny with black, coarse, straight hair.
- He sees things differently to others, such as appreciating the beauty of the **'candle buds'** when he, Jack and Ralph explore the island.
- He is kind: he stands up for Piggy when Jack says he didn't contribute to the fire. Simon points out that it was Piggy's glasses that were used to light it.

How does Simon's character develop?

- **Chapter Three**: Simon is the only one to help Ralph build the third shelter. We also see him assisting littluns by getting fruit down for them.
- **Chapter Five**: He tries to tell the boys that their fear of the beast is just their awareness of the evil of humanity, but he lacks the means to express it. They misunderstand him.
- **Chapter Eight**: The pig's head threatens him when he is in a trance, confirming his beliefs that the evil on the island is in the boys.
- **Chapter Nine**: He attempts to tell the boys that the beast that has been seen is the parachutist, but this time Simon is mistaken for the beast himself, and is killed.

Five key quotations

1. Simon's solitude: 'Simon dropped the screen of leaves back into place.' (Chapter Three)

2. Simon about the beast: 'What's the dirtiest thing there is?' (Chapter Five)

3. Simon to Ralph: 'You'll get back all right. I think so, anyway.' (Chapter Seven)

4. Piggy about Simon: 'He's cracked.' (Chapter Eight)

5. Simon about the beast: 'The beast was harmless and horrible; and the news must reach the others as soon as possible.' (Chapter Nine)

Note it!

Simon's death represents savagery overcoming civilisation, and a peak of violence from which it seems the boys cannot return. As Simon symbolises wisdom, perhaps spiritual wisdom, putting him to death shows the boys reaching a level of barbarity that changes them all.

Exam focus

How can I write about Simon's presentation in the novel? AO1

You can comment on how Golding presents Simon as mystical.

Golding continually shows Simon to be a mystery to the other boys. In the middle of the novel, Simon confounds Ralph by telling him, 'You'll get back all right. Ralph responds to this with a joke, but is clearly confused by Simon's apparent certainty. Golding uses the suddenness of Simon's comment to present him as odd or 'batty'.

Topic sentence clearly highlights character

Relevant quotation is fluently embedded

Shows strong textual knowledge

Explains how presentation contributes to character

Now you try!

Finish this paragraph about Simon's role in the novel. Use one of the quotations from the list.

Golding presents Simon as having greater understanding than the other boys when they discuss the nature of the beast. However ....

Five key things about Roger

1. **Roger** is **cruel** and **sadistic**.
2. He is **Jack's henchman**.
3. He enjoys **violence** and, in the end, is more **savage** even than **Jack**.
4. He is the one to **kill Piggy**.
5. He is the one with the **stick sharpened 'at both ends'** to get **Ralph**.

What are the first things we learn about Roger?

- No-one knows him.
- He is **'furtive'** (or secretive in a suspicious way) and keeps to himself.
- He deliberately kicks over the littluns' sandcastles, getting sand in Percival's eye, and messes up their game.
- He has black hair.
- He hides behind a tree to throw stones around Henry, but not directly at him.

How does Roger's character develop?

- **Chapter Four**: He is the first person Jack shows his mask to.
- **Chapter Six**: He wants to stay and roll rocks when they discover Castle Rock on the hunt for the beast.
- **Chapter Seven**: He goes up the mountain with Jack and Ralph.
- **Chapter Ten**: Roger appreciates Jack's leadership as **'proper'** because of its violence.
- **Chapter Eleven**: He throws stones at Piggy when he and Ralph challenge Jack over stealing the glasses, then levers a rock onto him with **'delirious abandonment'**.
- **Chapter Twelve**: Roger is portrayed as more dangerous than Jack; Samneric tell Ralph that he has a sharpened stick ready for him.

Five key quotations

1. Cruelty: 'Roger led the way straight through the castles, kicking them over, burying the flowers, scattering the chosen stones.' (Chapter Four)
2. Civilisation still rules him, but only just: 'Roger's arm was conditioned by a civilisation that knew nothing of him and was in ruins.' (Chapter Four)
3. Hunting: 'One piglet, with a demented shriek, rushed into the sea trailing Roger's spear behind it.' (Chapter Eight)
4. Piggy's murder: 'High overhead, Roger, with a sense of delirious abandonment, leaned all his weight on the lever' (Chapter Eleven)
5. Samneric to Ralph: ''You don't know Roger. He's a terror.' 'And the Chief —they're both—' '—terrors—' '—only Roger—' (Chapter Twelve)

Note it!

Roger can be viewed as representing figures like those around leaders such as Hitler and Stalin, who carried out atrocities on their leader's commands.

Exam focus

How can I write about Roger in the early stages of the novel? AO1

You can comment on how Golding presents Roger as initially limited in his cruelty.

In the early, pre-savagery, chapters, Golding shows how Roger's cruelty is limited. When he throws stones at Henry, he deliberately misses, as his 'arm was conditioned by a civilisation that knew nothing of him and was in ruins'. Although the adult world beyond the island is at war and thus 'in ruins', its structures still have some control over Roger's behaviour at this point.

Topic sentence refers to specific stage in the novel

Incident summarised and quotation embedded

Explains quotation's meaning

Explains in more depth

Now you try!

Finish this paragraph about Roger later in the novel. Use one of the quotations from the list.

Golding shows how Roger gives way to savagery when the hunters track the ....

Five key things about Sam and Eric

1. **Sam** and **Eric** are **identical twins** who are **not treated as individuals**.
2. The twins' **names become blended** as the book goes on – from Sam and Eric to **Samneric**, symbolising their **lack of separateness**.
3. They see the **parachutist** first and believe it is the **beast**.
4. They are **loyal** to **Ralph**, but end up forced to be in **Jack's tribe**.
5. In the political **allegory**, they represent **ordinary people** who do not ultimately get a choice about who or what to support.

What is Sam and Eric's function in the novel?

- They represent the common people, which is why it is important they are viewed collectively.
- Their alikeness contributes to humour at the start of the novel, before things start to go wrong.
- They spread fear with their dramatic retelling of the beast's characteristics, intensified by their twinned voices.
- They show how powerful evil is – people do not have the power to make fully good choices.

How does Sam and Eric's character develop through the novel?

- **First half of the novel**: they are occasionally mentioned but do not have a key role in the action. They giggle together and seem happy on the island.
- **Chapter Six**: They show they have been affected by fear when the parachutist lands and they think it is the beast.
- **Chapter Ten**: Sam and Eric are the only bigger boys to stay with Ralph and Piggy when everyone else goes with Jack.
- **Chapters Eleven and Twelve**: They resist Jack as long as they can when he tries to make them join his tribe. They are tortured by Roger into joining. They still warn Ralph and help him avoid capture.

Five key quotations

1. Humour when Ralph first takes their names: 'Then he got muddled; the twins shook their heads and pointed at each other, and the crowd laughed.' (Chapter One)
2. Unity when describing the beast: 'By custom now one conch did for both twins, for their substantial unity was recognised.' (Chapter Six)
3. Loyalty to the conch group: 'Memory of the dance that none of them had attended shook all four boys convulsively.' (Chapter Ten)
4. Bravery when Jack captures them: 'You lemme go—' '—and me.' (Chapter Eleven)
5. Goodness and loyalty: 'Listen Ralph, never mind what's sense. That's gone.' (Chapter Twelve)

Note it!

Their names blending together also shows how Golding mirrors order and civilisation breaking down in language itself. The boys do not even bother to keep words separate and neat any more.

Exam focus

How can I write about Sam and Eric's role at the start of the novel? AO1

You can comment on how Golding uses Sam and Eric for humour at first.

> At the start of the novel, Golding uses the twins' identical appearance for humour. When Ralph is collecting names, he gets 'muddled', which is presented as comic: 'the twins shook their heads and pointed at each other and the crowd laughed'. Although it is clearly a light-hearted moment, and the twins are often confused, this approach to them as being a source of comedy is only possible in the early part of the novel.

- Topic sentence refers to specific point in text
- Relevant quotation is fluently embedded
- Engages with the novel's tone
- Begins to link to structure

Now you try!

Finish this paragraph about the twins later in the play. Use one of the quotations from the list above.

Samneric's role in the novel develops as they come to represent ordinary people. This is apparent when ....

CHARACTERS The littluns

Five key things about the littluns

1. Few **littluns** are named individually – they are treated as a **group**.
2. The **boy with the birthmark** stands out, so his death in the fire is noticeable.
3. **Littluns** are **barely civilised**, being ruled by **instinct** and their **appetite**, although at least some stay with the **conch group**.
4. They **fear the beast**.
5. **Littluns** do not really affect the plot. Their role is to **follow the older boys** and show the **effects** of their **disputes and pressures**.

What do we learn about the littluns at the start of the novel?

- Piggy is unable to make a list of littluns' names, as they do not keep still. So the older boys do not even know how many of them there are.
- It appears to be anonymous littluns who call out their initial support for Ralph as leader, instinctively trusting him because of his association with the **'trumpet-thing'**.
- The youngest seem to be about six years old.
- They are scared of a beast, a **'snake-thing'** that they believe lives in the forest, which the older boys find hard to believe in.

How do the littluns develop?

- **Chapter Four**: Several littluns bear Roger and Maurice's bullying.
- **Chapter Seven**: Jack jokes about using a littlun to simulate hunting.
- **Chapter Five**: They giggle at the assembly where Ralph **'put[s] things straight'**, until the topic of the beast is raised. Then littluns can contribute – first Phil, and then Percival, who is unable to communicate. They all cry in sympathy.
- **Chapters Six and Seven**: They stay behind, with Piggy to look after them, when the older boys go to look for the beast.
- **Chapters Nine and Twelve**: They are involved in Simon's death and the hunt for Ralph.

Five key quotations

1. Piggy (about taking names): 'How could I with them little 'uns running round like insects?' (Chapter Two)
2. Shared identity as Phil explains about the beast: 'He paused, and the littluns laughed in horrified sympathy.' (Chapter Five)
3. The fear: 'the hunters crept to the platform and the littluns whimpered as now they so frequently did.' (Chapter Eight)
4. Savagery in the lead-up to Simon's death: 'Some of the littluns started a ring on their own; and the complementary circles went round and round' (Chapter Nine)
5. Loss of civilisation: 'Percival Wemys Madison sought in his head for an incantation that had faded clean away.' (Chapter Twelve)

Note it!

Remember Golding's moral purpose in writing the novel, to show that the potential for evil is in us all. Showing young children acting savagely and responding only to their own needs and wishes is an effective way of addressing this purpose.

Exam focus

How can I write about the function of the littluns? AO1 AO2

You can comment on how Golding uses the littluns to show the effects of disorder.

From the very beginning, Golding presents the littluns as lacking order and discipline. When the fire burns out of control, Piggy defends his inability to 'take names', saying 'How could I with them little 'uns running round like insects?' The littluns are presented here as chaotic, with Golding's use of the simile 'like insects' emphasising their small size, their number, and Piggy's feeling of being out of control.

Clear topic sentence sets up argument

Relevant quotation is fluently embedded

Explains by linking to themes

Analyses in detail using literary terminology

Now you try!

Finish this paragraph about the littluns' function in a later episode. Use one of the quotations from the list.

Golding uses the littluns to show the effects of key themes such as fear, for example when a meeting is called ....

My progress Needs more work ☐ Getting there ☐ Sorted! ☐ 41

1. Look at this ideas map representing Ralph. Is there anything else you can add?

'Not even Ralph knew how a link between him and Jack had snapped and been fastened elsewhere.'

Leadership

- Voted Chief by all
- Diplomatic
- Associated with conch and meetings
- His rules are to help things work properly (hygiene, fairness)
- Focused on long-term goal of rescue

Friendships — Simon, Piggy, Jack

Democracy

- Uses conch for fair speaking turns
- Listens to littluns about the beast

RALPH

Is only deliberate victim of boys' full savagery

Order/Civilisation

Rules

Turns

Fairness

Savagery

Decline

- Begins to forget what fire is for
- Involved in Simon's death (but the only character to see it as 'murder')

Worries about length of hair/cleanliness

'eager to take a place in this demented but partly secure society'

'THINGS BREAKING UP'

2. Create your own ideas map for one of the other characters.

Quick quiz

Answer these quick questions about the characters in the novel.

1. Which character has red hair?
2. Who represents democracy?
3. Who is 'batty'?
4. Which characters kick over littluns' sandcastles?

5. What is Jack's last name?
6. What other character's full name do we know?
7. Who kills Piggy?
8. Who weeps 'for the end of innocence'?
9. Who paints his face?
10. Name three littluns.
11. Who decides to leave an offering for the beast?
12. Who is in the 'conch group'?
13. Who picks fruit for littluns?
14. Who falls off the log at assemblies?
15. Who knows how to blow the conch?
16. Which boys are twins?
17. Who does Ralph believe 'could think'?
18. Who talks to the Lord of the Flies?
19. Whose is the first death on the island?
20. Who represents dictator-style power, like communism?

Power paragraphs

Write a **paragraph** in response to **each of these questions**. For each, try to use **one quotation** you have learned from this section.

1. How does Golding present Jack as caught up by the hunt?
2. Why does Golding include the scenes with Percival Wemys Madison?

Exam practice

Re-read the section in Chapter Four, from when Jack is told about the ship (page 74) to the end of the chapter.

Why is this moment significant in the text as a whole? Write **two paragraphs** explaining your ideas. You could comment on:
- Jack's personality and values as revealed in this scene
- how this exchange affects the boys' relationships.

Five key things about the theme of good and evil

1. Golding clearly shows the **battle between good and evil** at work on the island.

2. The battle between good and evil is represented in the **rivalry** between the **conch group** and the **savages**.

3. The **beast** also symbolises evil on the island.

4. Good is represented by **Ralph, Piggy and Simon**, who believe in the right thing to do.

5. With increasing **savagery**, evil rises and would win if it weren't for the **naval officer's arrival**.

How is good presented in *Lord of the Flies?*

- The conch symbolises democracy, fairness and order, reminding boys of the decency of their home society.

- Ralph and Simon work to build shelters, and Ralph insists on a signal fire to bring about a rescue.

- The island is initially presented as a paradise.

- Simon symbolises pure good in many ways. He is genuinely kind, e.g. picking fruit for smaller boys and giving Piggy his meat when Jack excludes him.

- The conch group go to Jack to ask for Piggy's glasses back **'because what's right's right'**.

How does Golding present evil?

- The beast is the external symbol of evil in the novel, serving to frighten the boys. Simon recognises that this evil in fact exists inside them.

- Hints foreshadow problems on the island, e.g. the **'witch-like cry'** in the opening, and the storm before Simon's death – but any real cruelty or danger is brought about by the boys.

- Jack's ability to be cruel is shown from the start in his treatment of Piggy.

- All the boys are involved in mob-related violence that escalates through the novel: the game where Robert is hurt, Simon's death and the hunting of Ralph.

Five key quotations

1. The island as paradise: 'this is a good island' (Ralph, Chapter Two)
2. Simon's kindness: 'Simon found for them the fruit they could not reach' (Chapter Three)
3. The storm leading up to the murderous dance: 'The flickering light became brighter and the blows of the thunder were only just bearable' (Chapter Nine)
4. The nature of the beast: 'What I mean is ... maybe it's only us.' (Simon, Chapter Five)
5. Evil in Jack's tribe: 'Roger advanced upon them as one wielding a nameless authority.' (about Samneric, Chapter Eleven)

Note it!

Golding said that 'man produces evil as a bee produces honey' and the novel reveals his belief that evil lurks inside all humankind, even British schoolboys. Such beliefs were influenced by his experiences during the Second World War, which he saw as venting existing evil tendencies in humankind.

Exam focus

How does Golding explore good and evil? (AO1)

You can write about how Golding uses the boys to explore good and evil.

> Golding explores ideas of good and evil through the boys' dramatic battle against the forces of evil within themselves. He makes it very clear that all the problems the boys face are caused by them and rooted in their own inherent evil, shown most symbolically in the haunting figure of the beast. Simon comes closest to understanding this, stating 'maybe it's only us', but failing to make himself clear to the others.

Clear topic sentence sets up point
Focus clearly on author
Literary feature noted
Quotation embedded effectively
Further detail provided

Now you try!

Finish this paragraph about the theme. Use one of the quotations from the list.

Golding shows that good is only apparent in the earlier parts of the novel and in very few characters. For example, Simon's goodness is shown ....

THEMES Civilisation and savagery

Five key things about the theme of civilisation and savagery

1. The novel traces a **broad shift from civilisation to savagery**, but some of the boys are always more civilised than others.
2. The boys initially try to build an **ordered, civilised society** like the one they have come from.
3. The conch, the signal fire and Piggy's glasses are all **symbols** of civilisation.
4. The **mask** and the **pig's head** represent **savagery**.
5. As the boys become more savage, they **think less** for themselves.

How do the boys go from civilisation to savagery?

- **Chapter Four**: The mask of face paint liberates them from civilised behaviour.
- **Chapter Five**: Rules such as those about toileting and guarding the fire are broken.
- The boys are increasingly less able to think ahead – they ignore the signal fire, kill a sow with piglets and burn down the fruit trees when hunting Ralph.
- Mob violence becomes increasingly serious: Robert is hurt, Simon killed accidentally and Ralph hunted.

How are ideas about civilisation and savagery presented?

- Symbols of civilisation and order are given great importance by Ralph, Piggy and Simon but are disrespected by Jack and his tribe.
- **Chapter Seven**: The boys' attitudes towards their physical appearance show their feelings about civilisation, e.g. Ralph's long hair and dirtiness trouble him.
- **Chapters Nine and Ten**: Even Ralph and Piggy are caught up in the **'dance'** that kills Simon, and Ralph begins to forget why the fire matters, showing he is losing touch with civilisation too.
- **Chapter Ten**: Language choices highlight the boys' relationship to civilisation, e.g. Jack's group is **'the tribe'** and members of it are called **'savages'**.
- The most violent scenes are presented as tribal, e.g. using hunting chants.

Five key quotations

1. The freedom of savagery: 'the mask was a thing on its own, behind which Jack hid, liberated from shame and self-consciousness.' (Chapter Four)
2. Jack's reverence of the beast: 'When we kill we'll leave some of the kill for it. Then it won't bother us, maybe.' (Chapter Eight)
3. Hunting chant: '*Kill the beast! Cut his throat! Spill his blood!*' (Chapter Nine)
4. Mob violence: 'There were no words, and no movements but the tearing of teeth and claws.' (Chapter Nine)
5. Symbols – Jack after Piggy's death: 'The conch is gone—' (Chapter Eleven)

Note it!

The only boy not to be savage in any way is Simon. This may be because he is intended to represent a higher and more spiritual way of thinking and being in the world.

Exam focus

How does Golding present ideas about civilisation and savagery? AO1 AO2

You can write about how Golding explores savagery through his language choices.

Golding describes the boys using language associated with savagery in the second half of the novel. For example, when they kill Simon, Golding states 'There were no words', implying that their lack of language shows a lack of humanity. He also describes the 'tearing of teeth and claws' using nouns that are normally associated with predators rather than people.

> Topic sentence identifies language as focus and specifies part of the novel

> Quotation is contextualised

> Explains implications clearly

> Zooms in using linguistic terminology

> Further explanation adds detail

Now you try!

Finish this paragraph about civilisation and savagery. Use one of the quotations from the list.

Golding explores the ease with which boys slip from a civilised state to a state of savagery. An example that suggests the boys enjoy descending into savagery comes when Jack paints his face ....

THEMES Power and leadership

Five key things about the theme of power and leadership

1. **Power** is initially organised by means of a **vote** for a chief, which **Ralph** easily wins.

2. Jack **requests that he be chief** (Ralph never does) and **challenges** Ralph's power directly several times throughout the novel.

3. Ralph takes his leadership **responsibilities** seriously.

4. Ralph and Jack represent **opposite approaches** to leadership: **democracy** and **dictatorship**.

5. At times, **physical power** is contrasted with **mental power** on the island, with physical force (violence) ultimately overtaking the boys.

How is power distributed on the island?

- Ralph wins the leadership vote, seemingly due to his association with the conch. While the boys are more civilised, they will listen to rational plans.

- Jack gradually takes power, as hunting becomes more attractive to the boys. As savagery overcomes them, their instincts rule them more.

- As fear of the beast becomes more immediate, Jack manipulates this fear by emphasising his physical skills as a hunter.

- The boys effectively switch from following the symbolic power of the conch to the more straightforward power of physical violence.

What different ideas about leadership are presented?

- Ralph represents a democratic approach to leadership. He wins by a fair vote, and allows everyone a voice by means of the conch.

- Ralph institutes rules that are for the good of the whole group and are focused on long-term goals such as shelter and rescue.

- Jack represents a dictatorial approach to leadership. He believes he should be chief because he held power with the choir previously.

- Jack's reasons for rules make little logical sense and his focus as a leader is on providing fun and meat, both short-term goals. He controls by physical force.

Five key quotations

1. Rules: 'We've got to have rules and obey them. [...] We're English; and the English are best at everything. So we've got to do the right things.' (Jack, Chapter Two)

2. Ralph taking leadership seriously: 'This meeting must not be fun, but business.' (Chapter Five)

3. Jack's views on what makes a leader: 'You can't hunt, you can't sing—' (Chapter Five)

4. Jack exploits fear of the beast: 'If there's a beast, we'll hunt it down! We'll close in and beat and beat and beat—!' (Chapter Five)

5. Robert about Jack's means of control: 'He got angry and made us tie Wilfred up.' (Chapter Ten)

Note it!

Note that Piggy and Roger are key to understanding Ralph and Jack's leadership styles. Without Piggy's ideas and, later, his reminders about the fire's purpose, Ralph would not be such an effective leader. Similarly, without Roger's aid in the form of violence, Jack's leadership would be weaker.

Exam focus

How does Golding present aspects of power? AO1

You can write about how Golding shows Jack's misuse of power.

Golding shows the dangers of the physical overtaking the mental and/or spiritual, for example the boys under Jack are ruled through physical force. Near the end of the novel, Jack beats Wilfred but the reasons are unclear or seemingly unimportant – the information worth passing on was only that Jack 'got angry and made us tie Wilfred up', not about what Wilfred did. This shows how the boys are at the mercy of Jack's somewhat unpredictable reactions.

Topic sentence makes point clearly

Explanation of point

Quotation is embedded

Idea is developed

Now you try!

Finish this paragraph about leadership. Use one of the quotations from the list.

Golding uses Ralph and Jack to present opposing ideas about leadership. This is clear when ....

THEMES Fear and the beast

Five key things about the themes of fear and the beast

1. Fear starts with the **littluns**, who talk first about a **'snake-thing'**.
2. The older boys first try to argue **rationally** that a beast could **not possibly exist** on the island.
3. The boys' **irrational fears**, as they move further away from **civilisation**, make them perceive a beast when the body of the **parachutist** lands on the island.
4. Jack **manipulates the boys' fears** to emphasise the importance of **physical strength and hunting**.
5. Reactions to the beast highlight the boys' **essential differences**.

How do the boys respond to fear?

- The littluns' fears are primal (the most basic): they are scared of vague creatures that lurk in the night. The older boys try to console them with logic.
- During the meeting to **'decide about the fear'**, Piggy considers fear of people – a far more rational fear.
- Simon recognises that the evil to be feared lies inside the boys themselves, but cannot explain this clearly enough to the others.
- Jack talks about feeling something watching in the forest and later makes his hunters appease the beast by leaving it an offering from their kill.

How does Golding present the beast?

- The beast **symbolises** evil, which at first seems to be like a monster.
- The parachutist seems to arrive as a requested sign from the world of grown-ups, and is immediately taken for the beast – a beast in human, broken, adult form.
- The beast is also presented through the **'Lord of the Flies'** – a translated form of the demon name **'Beelzebub'**, given to the pig's head.
- The **'Lord of the Flies'** points out that the beast cannot be defeated by physical means, and makes a clear link between evil and giving in to pleasure.

THEMES Fear and the beast

Five key quotations

1. Rational argument from Ralph: 'You couldn't have a beastie, a snake-thing, on an island this size.' (Chapter Two)
2. Fear: 'but I know there isn't no fear, either [...] Unless we get frightened of people.' (Piggy, Chapter Five)
3. Nature of the beast: 'What's the dirtiest thing there is?' (Simon, Chapter Five)
4. The beast as undefeatable: 'Fancy thinking the Beast was something you could hunt and kill!' (Lord of the Flies, Chapter Eight)
5. Evil as giving in to desires: 'We are going to have fun on this island!' (Lord of the Flies, Chapter Eight)

Note it!

Note that when they have the meeting in Chapter Five, Ralph encourages everyone to **'decide about the fear'** and is shocked when Jack lectures the littluns for being afraid. This clearly shows the difference in their approaches to leadership, even at this early stage.

Exam focus

How does Golding use the concept of the beast? AO1

You can write about the beast as a symbol for evil.

Golding uses the beast as a symbol for evil throughout the novel, but the scene where Simon communicates with the Lord of the Flies highlights a number of key aspects. The beast's non-physical nature, making it impossible to 'hunt and kill' it, is chief among these. The importance of this is shown when the pig's head mocks Simon, saying 'Fancy thinking the beast was something you could hunt and kill!'

- Topic sentence to summarise key idea
- Detail locates scene
- Quotation detail fluently embedded
- Detailed explanation with full quotation

Now you try!

Finish this paragraph about the beast. Use one of the quotations from the list.

Golding uses the beast to highlight differences between the characters, as they respond differently to it. This is clear when Ralph ....

My progress   Needs more work ☐   Getting there ☐   Sorted! ☐   51

THEMES Friendship

Five key things about the theme of friendship

1. Friendship is presented as something that can be **won** or **lost** on the island.
2. Piggy clearly **seeks Ralph's friendship** at the start, while others seem less focused on this as a goal.
3. Ralph's **allegiance** is clearly shown as **transferring** from Jack to Piggy.
4. The **littluns** seem to have undefined alliances, which suits their **less civilised** starting position.
5. It is clear that some boys (e.g. the choir, Samneric) **knew each other** before arriving on the island, but **most do not**.

What friendships do we see on the island?

- Piggy's initial attempts to make friends with Ralph are ignored, and his feelings are hurt when Ralph reveals his nickname. Their friendship only really begins after the signal fire argument in Chapter Four.

- Jack and Ralph form a friendship through shared experiences of exploring, but their differing values are soon exposed and make this unsustainable.

- Simon is the only boy we see actively seeking time alone, but he does also treat everyone as a potential friend – although others do not all respond to this, seeing him as weird.

- Samneric have a genuine, close bond, e.g. speaking as one, and are treated as a single unit.

How does Ralph and Piggy's friendship develop?

- **Chapter One**: Piggy clearly tries to be friends immediately, but Ralph does not really notice. Piggy tries to exchange names, but Ralph does not ask his.
- **Chapter Four**: Ralph teases Piggy over his invention plans. Piggy is still trying to be Ralph's friend, but by the end of this chapter, with Jack letting the fire out and smashing Piggy's glasses, Ralph's loyalties shift.
- **Chapter Five**: Piggy and Ralph, with Simon, are united against Jack's chaos.
- **Chapter Ten**: Ralph changes his story about Simon's death to match Piggy's inability to face it.

Five key quotations

1. Simon and Ralph: 'When they had done laughing, Simon stroked Ralph's arm shyly; and they had to laugh again.' (Chapter One)
2. Jack and Ralph: 'Ralph found himself alone on a limb with Jack and they grinned at each other, sharing this burden.' (Chapter Two)
3. Ralph teasing Piggy: 'Piggy saw the smile and misinterpreted it as friendliness.' (Chapter Four)
4. Ralph's loyalties: 'Not even Ralph knew how a link between him and Jack had snapped and been fastened elsewhere.' (Chapter Four)
5. Piggy linked to Ralph – about Jack: 'He can't hurt you: but if you stand out of the way he'd hurt the next thing. And that's me.' (Chapter Five)

Note it!

Note that the book ends with Ralph mourning the loss of Piggy, described as **'the true, wise friend called Piggy'**. Friendship is not centralised as a theme in the novel, but it is Ralph's closing thought.

Exam focus

How does Golding explore the theme of friendship? AO1 AO2

You can write about how Simon presents the theme of friendship.

> Golding explores one approach to friendship through Simon. Although often described as 'batty' and clearly an outsider, in the opening chapter Golding shows how he 'stroked Ralph's arm shyly'. This suggests a desire for friendship, with the use of the adverb 'shyly' implying that Simon is uncertain about how this will be received.

- Clear topic sentence states point
- Useful integration of brief additional quotation
- Quotation embedded effectively
- Clear explanation
- Clear explanation

Now you try!

Finish this paragraph about friendship. Use one of the quotations from the list.

Golding shows how Ralph and Piggy's friendship develops through the novel, based on shared experiences and values that they have in common. For example, when …

Five key things about the themes of nature and religion

1. The island setting can be seen as a **paradise before the boys' arrival**. The boys' **plane** literally **scars the jungle**.

2. **Nature provides** for the boys, in the form of fresh water, fruit and edible animals, but the boys do not make the best use of these.

3. **Religion** is another way in which boys can be more **civilised**, or more **savage**, in their practices.

4. Simon engages in a kind of **meditative practice**, supporting his presentation as a **prophet figure**.

5. The savages' practice of leaving **offerings** for the beast refers to rituals from **ancient religions**.

How is nature presented as significant in the novel?

- The sheer amount of description given to nature shows its importance. Golding details the landscape, the trees and wildlife, to ensure that readers understand the island as a tropical paradise.

- Golding reveals through his language choices that the island is damaged by the boys.

- The storm building up to Simon's death plays a crucial part in this event, eventually washing away the bodies.

- Gifts provided by nature are not well-used by the boys once they become savage, for example killing the sow.

How are religion and belief explored in the novel?

- Simon can be seen as a Christ-like figure. His ability to see the true nature of the beast (evil) is what leads to his death.

- Simon seeks solitude and performs a type of meditation, enabling him to commune with nature.

- Jack's tribe practise a primitive kind of religion by seeking to appease the beast with offerings, to avoid disaster.

- Ralph's request for a sign from the outside world, answered by the arrival of the parachutist, brings a new belief in a physical beast.

Five key quotations

1. Piggy on wasting nature's gifts: 'Now you been and set the whole island on fire.' (Chapter Two)

2. Simon at peace in nature: 'he was in a little cabin screened off from the open space by a few leaves.' (Chapter Three)

3. Ralph asking for a sign: 'If only they could send us something grown-up … a sign or something.' (Chapter Five)

4. The offering: 'The silence accepted the gift and awed them.' (Chapter Eight)

5. The effect of the storm: 'The dark sky was shattered by a blue-white scar.' (Chapter Nine)

Note it!

Golding portrays nature as powerful and worthy of respect. When the boys ignore or forget this, such as not preparing for storms by building shelters, it is a sign of their growing distance from civilisation.

Exam focus

How does Golding present nature? AO2

You can write about how Golding uses nature to create atmosphere.

Golding uses natural settings to build tension and contribute to atmosphere. For example, leading up to Simon's death, the sound and drama of the storm is incorporated into the rhythm of the dance: 'The dark sky was shattered by a blue-white scar.' Here, Golding presents the storm violently, using harsh consonants and short vowel sounds to add to the vicious and ritualistic dance.

Topic sentence explains overall point

Quotation is contextualised and explained

Focus on language use

Further explanation

Now you try!

Finish this paragraph about religion. Use one of the quotations from the list above.

Golding portrays the boys acting on belief in different ways in the novel, using the idea of religion to highlight their characters and their descent into savagery. For example, Ralph's wish ....

My progress Needs more work ☐ Getting there ☐ Sorted! ☐ 55

1. Look at this ideas map representing the theme of the beast. Is there anything else you can add?

2. Create your own ideas map for one of the other themes.

Quick quiz

Answer these quick questions about the novel's themes.

1. What are the symbols of civilisation?

2. What are the boys scared of?

3. Which theme(s) does the signal fire symbolise?
4. Which two boys are the main power struggles between?
5. How do the huts relate to the theme of civilisation?
6. Who is shown engaging in religious practices?
7. What is the Lord of the Flies?
8. What style of leadership does Ralph represent?
9. What do Samneric think is the beast?
10. Why does it matter that the hunters kill a sow with piglets?
11. Which boy introduces the mask?
12. What does the mask represent?
13. What is 'a link … had snapped and been fastened elsewhere' referring to?
14. Who is killed along with the conch, and what does this signify?
15. Who is the most 'good' of the characters?
16. Whose friendship does Ralph leave behind for Piggy's?
17. Why is it significant that Roger throws stones 'to miss' Henry?
18. What kind of leadership does Jack represent?
19. How does the pig's head relate to the theme of savagery?

Power paragraphs

Write **a paragraph** in response to **each of these questions**. For each, try to use **one quotation** you have learned from this section.

1 How do the boys try to create a civilised society at the start of the novel?
2 How does Golding use the natural world to highlight the theme of evil?

Exam practice

Re-read the section at the end of Chapter Eight where Simon is communicating with the Lord of the Flies.

Why is this moment significant in the text as a whole? Write **two paragraphs** explaining your ideas. You could comment on:

● ideas about evil and the beast
● ideas about friendship.

LANGUAGE Voice and dialogue

Five key things about voice and dialogue

1. Golding uses a **third person** omniscient narrator, so the reader sees what all the boys are doing and thinking, **without a single character's biased view**.

2. The narrator can **convey the boys' behaviour and motivations** with more understanding than they themselves have.

3. Using the **third person** allows Golding to include **descriptive detail** of the setting and of the boys and their actions.

4. He uses colloquial language in dialogue, showing how the boys would really speak.

5. He uses specific types of language (e.g. standard/non-standard English) for different boys' **dialogue to show character**.

How does Golding develop theme using narrative voice?

- Switching between different characters' perspectives shows us, for example, the different rate of descent into savagery when Jack is hunting while Ralph is trying to finish the huts. (Chapter Three)

- Golding chooses vocabulary to emphasise theme, e.g. describing Jack as **'like an idol'** when Piggy and Ralph go to the tribe. (Chapter Nine)

How does Golding use dialogue to develop character?

- Piggy's speech is intended as representative of lower-class language, to make him stand out. He uses non-standard rather than standard English, e.g. **'I didn't expect nothing'**. (Chapter One)

- Jack's speech can be aggressive, e.g. **'Shut up, Fatty'** (Chapter One), whereas Ralph swears only when provoked.

How does Golding use narrative voice to develop the setting?

- Extended descriptions precede many events, with strong verbs and detailed noun phrases, e.g. the bird **'flashed'** with a **'witch-like cry'**. (Chapter One)

- The omniscient narration allows for changes in the narrative, e.g. to introduce the storm in Chapter Nine: **'Over the island the build-up of clouds continued.'**

Five key quotations

1. Narrative voice to create the setting in Simon's clearing: 'The candle-buds opened their wide white flowers glimmering under the light that pricked down from the first stars.' (Chapter Three)

2. Narrative voice to develop theme while hunting the beast: 'Their footsteps and the occasional breeze were stirring up small devils of dust.' (Chapter Seven)

3. Colloquial dialogue portrays the boys' excitement: 'Wacco!' (Chapter Two)

4. Dialect to create character: 'Aren't I having none?' (Piggy, Chapter Four)

5. Harsh language in dialogue, e.g. to show emotion: 'You're a beast and a swine and a bloody, bloody thief' (Ralph to Jack, Chapter Eleven)

Note it!

Golding's use of an omniscient narrator allows him the option to comment on the boys' actions, but he avoids this. Instead, he presents events directly, allowing the reader to judge. The reader has to mostly infer moral points rather than have them explained.

Exam focus

How can I write about Golding's use of dialogue? AO2

You can use Piggy to write about Golding's use of dialogue.

Golding develops Piggy's character through his careful use of language. His outcry to Jack of 'Aren't I having none?' shows his typical lower-class speech compared to the other boys. The use of 'none' creates a double negative, which is non-standard grammatically. Golding wants the reader, like the other boys, to see Piggy as different in his speech as well as in his physique and attitudes.

| Overall point about character |
| Evidence |
| Analysis of language use |
| Summative point links to other characters |

Now you try!

Finish this paragraph about Golding's use of narrator. Use one of the quotations from the list.

Golding uses the third person omniscient narrative voice to support thematic ideas even when describing actions and setting. For example, when the boys were hunting ......

LANGUAGE Writer's effects

Five key things about writer's effects in the novel

1. As *Lord of the Flies* is allegorical, symbolism is crucial. **Key objects**, e.g. the **conch, Piggy's glasses**, the **fire** and even characters, act as symbols.
2. Golding uses irony, often to highlight differences between the way things are, and the way they 'should be'.
3. There are many examples of simile and metaphor, particularly in **descriptive** passages.
4. Foreshadowing **warns readers**, as well as **the boys**, of imminent **danger**.
5. Golding's **descriptions** of the **settings** are **rich and evocative**.

How does Golding use symbolism to develop themes?

- The conch, symbol of democracy and civilisation, remains powerful – from Ralph's election through association to it, to Piggy's faith in it when approaching Jack at the end.
- Fire operates as a symbol of hope for rescue, and of civilisation, but also of savagery when it burns down large parts of the forest.

How does Golding use irony in the novel?

- Golding uses a kind of dramatic irony, where a character's words are appreciated differently by the reader, e.g. with the naval officer at the end: **'Jolly good show. Like the Coral Island.'**
- He also uses situational irony, a mismatch between a situation and the consequences to which it leads. For example, the boys are 'rescued' through a fire started by Jack.

How does Golding use foreshadowing to strengthen themes?

- Golding shows the boys' increasing savagery, e.g. in the hunting game which moves from harmlessness to hurt. This also foreshadows Simon's fate.
- Metaphors also highlight themes – when Roger throws stones the first time, he is held back by **'the squatting protection of parents and school and policemen and the law'**. Later, civilisation does not stop him.

Five key quotations

1. Simile to create tone (about sunlight): 'One patch touched a tree trunk and scrambled up like a bright squirrel.' (Chapter Two)

2. Metaphor to add character detail: 'Passions beat about Simon on the mountain-top with awful wings.' (Chapter Four)

3. Symbolism focusing on a theme, or supporting allegory: 'I thought they wanted the conch.' (Piggy, Chapter Ten)

4. Irony to support allegory: 'What have you been doing? Having a war or something?' (naval officer, Chapter Twelve)

5. Foreshadowing to emphasise themes: 'Ralph too was fighting to get near, to get a handful of that brown, vulnerable flesh.' (Chapter Seven)

Note it!

Golding's descriptions are rich through his use of vivid vocabulary, e.g. when Ralph is first looking around the island: 'Beyond the platform there was more enchantment.' The noun 'enchantment' precisely conveys the atmosphere and tone Golding wishes to create.

Exam focus

How can I write about Golding's use of imagery? AO2

You can write about use of metaphor to explore Golding's imagery.

Golding develops Simon's character through metaphor. When Jack breaks Piggy's glasses, 'Passions beat about Simon … with awful wings' showing how strongly he feels in that moment. The metaphor suggests that Simon is experiencing multiple conflicting feelings, and that they are difficult to handle. Golding shows how Simon is kind to Piggy, as he retrieves the glasses, but also suggests that he is scared of Jack himself.

- Overall point about character
- Evidence
- Analysis of language use
- Summative point links to other characters

Now you try!

Finish this paragraph about language and allegory. Use one of the quotations from the list above.

Golding chooses language features to support the allegorical meanings created in the novel. For example, when Jack attacks Ralph's group ....

My progress Needs more work ☐ Getting there ☐ Sorted! ☐ 61

Five key things about the exam

1. You need to answer **one** question from a **choice of two** on *Lord of the Flies*.

2. It will focus on **Golding's exploration** of an aspect of the novel, such as a **character**, **relationship** or **theme**, and how he **presents** it.

3. You will have about **45–50 minutes** to read and respond to the question.

4. There are **30 marks** for the question, which assesses **AOs 1, 2 and 3**. Remember that **AO3** relates to **'context'**.

5. You can also gain a further **4 marks** for **AO4**: your use of **spelling, punctuation and grammar**.

What will a question look like?

1. How far does Golding present Piggy as a sympathetic character in the novel?

Write about:

- what Piggy says and does in the novel
- how far Golding presents Piggy as a sympathetic character.

[30 marks]

AO4 [4 marks]

You must make your own judgement

You must explain or analyse the techniques Golding uses

These are the aspects you must tackle

A reminder to watch use of spelling, punctuation, vocabulary and grammar

Do all questions look the same?

- Not all questions will begin this way. Some might contain **statements** you must argue with or against. For example, 'Golding shows how the children in *Lord of the Flies* are no more innocent than the adults at war in the world beyond the island.' How far do you agree with this statement?

- Some questions might ask you about a **relationship** between two characters, e.g. between Ralph and Jack.

What do I need to do to get a good mark?

Use this grid to understand what your current level is and how to improve it:

	AO1 Read, understand, respond	**AO2** Analyse language, form, structure and effects	**AO3** Show understanding of context
High	• You make **precise references** to the question focuses. • Your argument is **well-structured**, with quotations **fluently embedded** in sentences.	• You **analyse** and **interpret** the methods Golding uses **very effectively**. • You **explore thoughtfully** the effects of these on the reader. • You show **excellent use** of subject terminology.	• You make **detailed, relevant links** between specific elements of the novel and its **social, historical contexts**.
Mid	• You make a **range of references** to the focuses of the question. • You respond in a **clear, logical way** with **relevant quotations** chosen.	• You **explain clearly** some of the methods Golding uses, and **some effects** on the reader. • You use **mostly relevant** subject terminology.	• You show **clear evidence** of understanding context, which is **linked** to the novel in places.
Lower	• You make **some references** to the focus of the question, but in rather a patchy way. • You make **some useful points** but evidence is **not always clear**.	• You make **occasional attempts** to explain Golding's methods but these are a little **unclear**. • You show **some use** of subject terminology.	• You demonstrate **basic awareness** of context but **links** to the novel are **undeveloped** and **not always relevant**.

AO4 For top marks: use a **range** of vocabulary and sentence structures, adopt a **clear, purposeful and effective** writing style, and make sure your spelling and punctuation are **accurate**.

Read these exam-style single character questions

2. How does Golding use Jack's destructive nature to explore conflict in the novel?

   Write about:
   - how Jack speaks and behaves in the novel
   - how Golding uses Jack to explore ideas about conflict.

   [30 marks] AO4 [4 marks]

3. 'I'm chief. I'll go. Don't argue.' How far does Golding present Ralph as being brave?

   Write about:
   - what Ralph does and says in the novel
   - how Golding presents Ralph as brave.

   [30 marks] AO4 [4 marks]

4. 'Simon is the only truly good character on the island.' How do you view Golding's presentation of Simon?

   Write about:
   - how Simon speaks and behaves in the novel
   - how Golding uses Simon to explore ideas about morality.

   [30 marks] AO4 [4 marks]

5. How does Golding present Piggy as a 'true, wise friend'?

   Write about:
   - what Piggy does and says in the novel
   - how Golding presents Piggy as a friend.

   [30 marks] AO4 [4 marks]

NOW read these further character questions

These questions deal with **relationships** between characters or how the author presents some characters in **different ways** from others:

6. How does Golding present the changing relationship between Ralph and Jack over the course of the novel?

   Write about:
   - how they speak to and behave towards each other
   - how Golding presents their relationship through the way he writes.

   [30 marks] AO4 [4 marks]

7. How does Golding reveal Jack and Piggy's differences through their responses to the survival situation?

   Write about:
   - how they respond to the situation through their speech and actions
   - how Golding presents their differences through the way he writes.

   [30 marks] AO4 [4 marks]

8. How does Golding present Ralph and Piggy's changing relationship throughout the novel?

   Write about:
   - how they speak and behave towards each other
   - how Golding presents their relationship through the way he writes.

   [30 marks] AO4 [4 marks]

Five key stages to follow

1. **Read** the **question** and **highlight** key words.
2. Quickly **generate ideas** for your response.
3. **Plan** for paragraphs.
4. **Write** your response; **check it** against your plan as you progress.
5. **Check** for **AO4** as you progress (spelling, punctuation, vocabulary, etc.).

What do I focus on?

Highlight the key words:

> 2. How does Golding use Jack's destructive nature to explore conflict in the novel?
>
> Write about:
> - how Jack speaks and behaves in the novel
> - how Golding uses Jack to explore ideas about conflict.
>
> **[30 marks] AO4 [4 marks]**

What do they tell you? Focus on the novel as a whole; explain what specific methods Golding uses; stick to how Jack's destructive nature shows conflict, as the main topic.

How do I get my ideas?

Note your ideas in a spider diagram or list them in a table:

How he speaks and behaves

how he speaks:

aggressive speech: 'Shut up, Fatty'

emphasises separation: 'my hunters'

how he behaves:

gets obsessed with hunting

hits Piggy and breaks glasses – doesn't apologise

Ideas about his destructive nature and conflict

conflict with Piggy from beginning

allegory: democracy/ dictatorship – hatred of conch, glee when destroyed

Jack as destructive

How he speaks and behaves	Ideas about his destructive nature and conflict
• Aggressive speech: 'shut up, Fatty' • Emphasises separation: 'my hunters' • Gets obsessed with hunting • Hits Piggy and breaks glasses – doesn't apologise	• Conflict with Piggy from beginning • Allegory: democracy/dictatorship – hatred of conch, glee when destroyed

How do I structure my ideas?

Make a **plan** for **paragraphs.*** Decide the order for your points:

- Paragraph 1: *Go straight into your first point: Jack shows destructive tendencies from the start – conflict with Piggy, aggressive speech.*
- Paragraph 2: Becomes more destructive as more obsessed with hunting, mask – link to theme and symbol.
- Paragraph 3: Challenges Ralph as leader, keeps talking about **'my hunters'**, to Ralph and Piggy (link to context – democracy/dictatorship).
- Paragraph 4: Piggy's death and conch's destruction.
- Paragraph 5: Golding shows destructiveness as savage and wasteful – sow, forest; Jack lost at end when naval officer arrives because civilisation destroyed.

How do I write effectively?

Write **clear**, **analytical** paragraphs and **embed** your evidence. For example:

Golding presents Jack as having destructive tendencies from the very beginning. This is clear in his conflict with Piggy, which Jack expresses through aggressive and unpleasant speech such as 'shut up, Fatty'. Golding develops this conflict between Jack and Piggy throughout the novel, setting them up as opposites: Piggy is a rational thinker, while Jack is instinctive, living in the moment.

Clear topic sentence	
Clear reference to question	
Embedded quotation	
Explanation of an idea	
Further detail	

Now you try!

Re-read Question 3 on page 64 and plan your response in the same way.

* The plan above and the sample answers on pages 68–71 have five paragraphs, but you don't need to be limited to this if you have more points to include (and time to write them!)

What does a Grade 5 answer look like?

Read the task again, then the sample answer below.

2. How does Golding use Jack's destructive nature to explore conflict in the novel?

Write about:

- how Jack speaks and behaves in the novel
- how Golding uses Jack to explore ideas about conflict.

[30 marks] AO4 [4 marks]

Jack is obviously destructive from the beginning of the book, as he acts like a bully towards Piggy. Golding shows how the two characters are in conflict with each other right from the start through Jack's use of aggressive language towards Piggy like 'shut up, Fatty.' He breaks Piggy's glasses hitting him and will not apologise, showing how angry and bitter he is.

AO1 Clear statement setting out viewpoint

AO2 Close reference to language and link to theme

Jack becomes obsessed with hunting and he seems at first to just want to kill a pig to prove he can, but after that he needs to just keep killing. Hunting is a good thing in some ways as it is useful, to provide them with food, but the way that Jack has a 'compulsion' to do it seems more about killing the animal than getting the meat to eat. This obsession also links to the symbol of the mask, which Golding introduces through Jack as a means of camouflage, and to highlight the key conflict between civilisation and savagery. The mask frees up Jack and the hunters to be savage, showing also how Golding links Jack's destructiveness with the theme of savagery. Jack's decline into savage behaviour contrasts strongly with typical adventure novels like 'The Coral Island' which is mentioned in the book, where the main characters remain civilised and bring 'modern' ideas to the island.

AO4 Sentences less well controlled here

AO2 Link to term but not developed

AO1 Clear developed explanation on theme and character

AO3 Comment on context with some detail

Jack's main conflict through the book is with Ralph. Jack wanted to be chief and he challenges Ralph's leadership a few times. He is destructive and tries to break up the group by trying to get other boys to follow him. Constantly emphasising 'my hunters' stops the group feeling united.

AO3 This paragraph feels rushed – needs developing

A key moment that shows Jack's destructiveness is Piggy's death. Although Jack does not kill Piggy himself, he reacts by 'screaming wildly', showing his delight and celebrating that 'The conch is gone'. Golding shows us how much Jack hates the conch, as a symbol of democracy, when he celebrates its destruction. Jack then also immediately viciously attacks Ralph by throwing a spear at him, showing that he is now freed to attack people. His destructiveness has turned towards humans, true to his role as a symbol for dictatorships like nazism or communism.

Paragraph 4

In the end, Golding uses Jack to show destructiveness as both savage and wasteful. Jack's destructive nature and savagery prevents him from planning ahead and thinking logically like Piggy, which leads him and his hunters to kill a sow with piglets. This shows thoughtlessness, as future meat is also being destroyed. Similarly, he sets fire to the entire forest just to force Ralph out to catch him, destroying all the fruit trees and also the wildlife. If they had not been rescued, they would not have had enough to eat. This shows how wasteful and pointless Jack's destructive attitude is.

Paragraph 5

Check the skills

Re-read paragraphs four and five of this response and:

- highlight other **points** made
- circle any reference to **context**
- underline any places where the student has made an **interpretation**.

Now you try!

Look again at paragraph three ('*Jack's main conflict…*', etc.) and improve it by doing the following:

- Adding a **reference or quotation** about Jack and Ralph to show them in conflict.
- **Explaining** how Jack **'challenges Ralph's leadership'** – provide an example or discuss in more detail.
- Ending with a **summary point** about the importance of **'my hunters'** to Jack and how this **language use** is significant.
- Improving the overall **style** by making sure your sentences **flow** – use **connectives** to **link** ideas.

EXAM PRACTICE Grade 7+ annotated sample answer

What does a Grade 7+ answer look like?

Read the task again, then the sample answer below.

2. How does Golding use Jack's destructive nature to explore conflict in the novel?

Write about:
- how Jack speaks and behaves in the novel
- how Golding uses Jack to explore ideas about conflict.

[30 marks] AO4 [4 marks]

Golding sows the seeds of Jack's destructive nature from the start. In the first assembly, Jack tells Piggy he is 'talking too much' and says, 'shut up, Fatty.' The aggression of this imperative towards a boy he has just met indicates confidence in his right to tell others what to do, and a lack of regard for others. These traits allow him to destroy what others build.

The island context feeds Jack's destructiveness through hunting. He quickly develops an unhealthy level of interest in hunting pigs, being unable to 'convey the compulsion to ... kill that was swallowing him up'. Golding here demonstrates how Jack is consumed by desire to kill through the metaphorical use of the verb 'swallowing'. In Jack's case, Golding shows hunting to be an addictive activity which is literally destructive in killing the pigs, but also metaphorically destroys Jack's humanity and creates conflict between him and Ralph. The symbol of the mask, which 'liberates' the boys from civilisation is a clear marker of this, contrasting with other representations of boys in the adventure genre such as 'The Coral Island'. Golding uses Jack to show that young boys could be capable of savagery.

Golding also shows Jack's destructive nature through his repeated challenges to Ralph's leadership. As well as explicit challenges, however, Jack's lack of commitment to unity is clear through his references to 'my hunters'. Using the possessive pronoun in this way presents this group as separate to the rest of the boys, encouraging division and making it far easier to create conflict.

AO1 Clear statement sets out argument

AO2 Carefully selected evidence and detailed analysis of language use and effect

AO1 Clear short sentence to show question focus

AO2 Strong language focus with effective terminology

AO3 Relevant and clear link to Golding's views

AO4 Connectives to link ideas and paragraphs

AO1 Clear sense of overview knowledge

AO2 Further detailed language analysis linked clearly to question focus

A key moment that illustrates Jack's destructive nature is Piggy's death. Jack celebrates the moment by shouting gleefully at Ralph, 'The conch is gone'. Golding focuses Jack's attention on the conch's destruction rather than on Piggy's death to highlight the symbolism of this moment. As Jack represents totalitarian leadership which, to Golding's contemporary readers would resonate most strongly as that practised by Stalin or Hitler, his joy at the destruction of a symbol of democracy works on the allegorical level to highlight the conflict between him and Ralph as symbols of different systems. Jack has consistently hated the conch, declaring it 'doesn't count' in different parts of the island and mocking Ralph and Piggy's devotion to it.

Paragraph 4

Finally, Golding shows how Jack's destructiveness leads to waste, which is in conflict with the model of preparedness shown by Ralph. Golding demonstrates how Ralph's focus on signal fires and shelters is practical and useful in their survival situation, while Jack's desire to hunt and kill ultimately burns up the entire forest, devastating everything – and could have cost the boys their lives.

Paragraph 5

Check the skills

Re-read paragraphs four and five of this response and:

- identify any particularly **fluent** or **well-expressed** ideas
- find any further references to **context**
- highlight any places where the student has shown **deeper insight** and offered **original** or particularly **thoughtful** ideas or made interesting **links**.

Now you try!

Now, using the plan you made for Question 3 on page 67, write a full response. Here's a reminder of the question:

3. 'I'm chief. I'll go. Don't argue.' How far does Golding present Ralph as brave?

   Write about:
   - what Ralph does and says in the novel
   - how Golding presents Ralph as brave.

   30 marks (plus 4 marks for AO4)

- Try to match your answer to the High Level objectives on page 63.

EXAM PRACTICE Theme questions

9. How does Golding use the novel to explore ideas about order and civilisation?

   Write about:
   - the way characters and events relate to ideas about order and/or civilisation
   - how Golding presents ideas about order and civilisation.

   [30 marks] AO4 [4 marks]

10. 'Of course we're frightened sometimes.' How does Golding use the idea of fear in the novel?

    Write about:
    - how different characters react to fear
    - how Golding uses fear to highlight different ideas.

    [30 marks] AO4 [4 marks]

11. How far do you agree that this is a novel of contrasts in its character, action and setting?

    Write about:
    - different contrasts shown in the novel
    - how Golding presents these contrasts by the way he writes.

    [30 marks] AO4 [4 marks]

12. 'He hates me. I dunno why.' What does Golding have to say about friendship in *Lord of the Flies*?

    Write about:
    - how the boys' friendships are formed and develop
    - how Golding explores these ideas in the way he writes.

    [30 marks] AO4 [4 marks]

NOW read these further theme questions

13. 'We're on an uninhabited island.' How does Golding use the setting to support the theme of savagery?

Write about:

● how Golding presents the setting

● how Golding explores ideas about savagery in the way he writes.

[30 marks] AO4 [4 marks]

14. How does Golding explore the significance of nature in the novel?

Write about:

● how nature is presented in the novel

● how Golding presents the significance of nature in the way he writes.

[30 marks] AO4 [4 marks]

15. How far do you agree that 'Lord of the Flies is a book about power struggles'?

Write about:

● how different characters seek and struggle for power

● how Golding presents these ideas as significant through the way he writes.

[30 marks] AO4 [4 marks]

Five key stages to follow

1. **Read** the **question** and **highlight** key words.
2. Quickly **generate ideas** for your response.
3. **Plan** for paragraphs.
4. **Write** your response; **check it** against your plan as you progress.
5. **Check** for **AO4** as you progress (spelling, punctuation, vocabulary, etc.).

What do I focus on?

9. How does Golding use the novel to explore ideas about order and civilisation?

   Write about:

   ● the way characters and events relate to ideas about order and/or civilisation

   ● how Golding presents ideas about order and civilisation.

   [30 marks] AO4 [4 marks]

What do they tell you? Focus on the play as a whole; explain what specific methods Golding uses; stick to the theme of order and civilisation as the main topic.

How do I get my ideas?

Note your ideas in a spider diagram or list them in a table:

Characters and events linked to ideas

Conch to speak – order in the boys' assemblies 'and he won't be interrupted'

Ralph & Piggy – represent order and civilisation and bring in civilised ideas

Order and civilisation

Golding's presentation

Symbolism – conch, Ralph/ Piggy, fire: 'Where the conch is, that's a meeting.'

Language and order (breaks down later) – little uns/littluns

Sam and Eric/Samneric

Different characters/events	Golding's presentation
• Conch to speak 'and he won't be interrupted'	• Symbolism – conch, fire: 'Where the conch is, that's a meeting.'
• Ralph & Piggy represent order and civilised ideas	• Language and order (breaks down later) 'littluns', 'Samneric'

HOW do I structure my ideas?

Make a **plan** for **paragraphs**.* Decide the order for your points:

- Paragraph 1: *Rules first establish order. e.g. conch gives the right to speech; practical rules such as where to toilet.*
- Paragraph 2: *Ralph and Piggy as linked to ideas of order and civilisation through being symbols of democracy.*
- Paragraph 3: *How language is linked to order through the breakdown shown in e.g. Sam and Eric's names and the little 'uns.*
- Paragraph 4: *The boys' attempts at having a civilised way of running things, such as using assemblies and rules and having specific roles, and how this links to the signal fire and may serve to keep them safe and help them be rescued.*
- Paragraph 5: *The naval officer's intervention at the end as a sign of how far the boys have come from civilisation – adults have to step in to save them.*

HOW do I write effectively?

Write **clear**, **analytical** paragraphs and **embed** your evidence. For example:

Golding shows the boys trying to establish order on the island through rules and systems, mostly copied from their experiences in civilised society. They remember 'hands up' at school and implement a rule of talking only when holding the conch, so that everyone can have a fair turn. This shows an attempt at creating an equal society at the start. They also set up practical rules such as filling coconut shells with water and only toileting in certain areas.	Overview point
	Quotation embedded in the sentence
	Clear link to theme in explanation
	Further details add weight to the initial point

Now you try!

Re-read Question 10 on page 72 and plan your response in the same way.

* The plan above and the sample answers on pages 76–79 have five paragraphs, but you don't need to be limited to this if you have more points to include (and time to write them!)

What does a Grade 5 answer look like?

Read the task again, then the sample answer below.

9. How does Golding explore ideas about order and civilisation?

Write about:

- the way characters and events relate to ideas about order and/or civilisation
- how Golding presents ideas about order and civilisation.

[30 marks] AO4 [4 marks]

Golding explores ideas about order and civilisation through the boys' attempts to manage on the island. At first, they set up a kind of society based on rules that are familiar to them from the civilised society they know. Having found the conch and used it to call the others, Ralph decides to use it to mark turns for talking: 'I'll give him the conch… And he won't be interrupted.' This shows the ordered society that Ralph wants to create, based on fairness.

Ralph is connected to order and civilisation throughout the novel. Golding uses allegory and symbolism in the novel and one of the allegorical systems is political, where Ralph represents democracy. This is shown by him being voted chief in a fair vote at the start, and then creating this fair system of anyone being able to speak in the assemblies if he is holding the conch. This links to the novel's context as Golding was writing during the Cold War period when people were aware of democracy as being opposed by the forces of communism. Piggy is also linked with order and civilisation, as he tends to bring the adult point of view to situations: 'what's grown-ups going to think?'.

Golding uses the novel's language to show how order breaks down. At the start, there are 'little 'uns', but by the end, they are 'littluns'. A similar thing happens to the twins' names, Sam and Eric which go to Samneric. Jack's tribe shows this too as the boys are called 'savages' and their chant is basic: 'Kill the beast! Cut his throat! Spill his blood!'

AO1 Clear statement setting out viewpoint

AO2 Comments on quotation, but analysis could be developed

AO2 Clearly addresses how Golding presents ideas

AO3 Sensible link to context

AO1 Clear explanation focused on question but quotation could be embedded

AO1 Relevant point but not fully explained

AO4 Expression not very clear – 'shorten' would be clearer

Golding shows that having a civilised way of running things gives the boys the best chance of safety and protection. The less civilised and more savage they become, they more danger they are in, and the less chance of rescue they have. I think Golding wants the reader to see that if they had all followed their roles, like if Jack hadn't 'let the bloody fire out', they would have been rescued much sooner. This shows that order is what could keep them safe, showing that a civilised (or democratic) society is safer than a savage (or communist) one.

Paragraph 4

The way the novel ends makes clear how far from civilisation the boys have come. The naval officer represents the civilised world coming back to rescue the boys and Golding uses him to show that the boys have got too savage to help themselves. Also, most of them are too far gone to even speak to him as they have left order so far behind. Jack tries to come forward, but stops himself and Percival Wemys Madison has forgotten even his personal details that earlier he was repeating like a chant.

Paragraph 5

Check the skills

Re-read paragraphs four and five of this response and:

- highlight other **points** made
- circle any reference to **context**
- underline any places where the student has made an **interpretation**.

Now you try!

Look again at paragraph three ('*Golding uses the novel's language…*') and improve it by doing the following:

- **Explaining** why '**littluns**' and '**Samneric**' show '**how order breaks down**'.
- **Explaining** what is 'basic' about the chant, and perhaps linking it to themes more clearly.
- Ending with a **summary point** about the importance of language through the novel.
- Improving the overall **style** by making sure your sentences **flow** and are **accurate** and **precise**; use connectives to **link** ideas.

What does a Grade 7+ answer look like?

Read the task again, then the sample answer below.

9. How does Golding explore ideas about order and civilisation?

Write about:

- the way characters and events relate to ideas about order and/or civilisation
- how Golding presents ideas about order and civilisation.

[30 marks] AO4 [4 marks]

Golding highlights ideas about order and civilisation from the start, with the boys initially seeking to create order on the island. This is shown through the adoption of rules which make their lives easier, such as 'I'll give him the conch… and he won't be interrupted.' Ralph's confidence, with the verb 'won't', shows faith in civilisation. However, Golding introduces the beginnings of conflict through Jack's relationship to order, as his enthusiasm for rules relates to being able to punish boys who break them, showing no understanding of the need for the rules themselves.

In fact, Ralph and Piggy are Golding's clearest character symbols of order and civilisation. In an allegorical reading, Ralph stands for democracy against Jack's dictatorship, shown through his usage of the conch to confer equality. As Golding was writing in the 1950s, when people saw fascism and communism as substantial threats, these meanings would be clear to contemporary readers. Piggy, however, symbolises civilisation through his intellect and use of adult reasoning: 'What's grown-ups going to think?'.

Golding also uses language in the novel to highlight the juxtaposition. As order gradually breaks down, so too does the boys' language. This is perhaps most evident in the phrase 'little 'uns', becoming the single word 'littluns', like Sam and Eric's identity, abbreviated to 'Samneric'. Breakdown in language mirrors the divisions in the boys' society, and can also be seen in the increasing simplicity of Jack's language and use of primitive chants like 'Kill the beast! Cut his throat! Spill his blood!'.

AO1 Clear statement sets out argument

AO2 Carefully selected evidence and analysis of language use and effect

AO2 Strong structural point showing contrast

AO4 Clear link between paragraphs

AO1 Point is developed and interpreted

AO3 Excellent knowledge of context linked to interpretations

AO1 Clear overview

AO2 Language use explained and linked to theme

Golding shows that being civilised would make life safer for the boys. Following the rules agreed at assemblies would protect them from the elements and from stomach problems, and help them be rescued. Golding also uses fire as a symbol to contrast civilisation and savagery: the signal fire represents an element utilised to benefit mankind. Fire, however, represents loss of order when it burns out of control at the start, and violent aggression when Jack smokes Ralph out at the end.

Paragraph 4

Ironically, it is this final savage fire that brings the naval officer to the island, but Ralph is the only boy left with enough civilisation to speak to an outsider. The naval officer functions as a new civilised lens to view the 'group of painted boys' through, as the reader has been until this point immersed in their experiences. His external judgement that a 'pack of British boys' should have 'put up a better show' shows how far from civilisation the boys have strayed.

Paragraph 5

Check the skills

Re-read paragraphs four and five of this response and:

1. identify any particularly **fluent** or **well-expressed** ideas
2. find any further references to **context**
3. highlight any places where the student has shown **deeper insight** and offered **original** or particularly **thoughtful** ideas or made interesting **links**.

Now you try!

Now, using the plan you made for Question 10 on page 75, write a full response. Here's a reminder of the question:

10. 'Of course we're frightened sometimes.' How does Golding use the idea of fear in the novel?

Write about:
- how different characters react to fear
- how Golding uses fear to highlight different ideas.

[30 marks] AO4 [4 marks]

- Try to match your answer to the High Level objectives on page 63.

Now you try!

Now, practise applying the skills you have learned to these **new questions**.

- Note down key points you wish to use.
- Select the key quotations you want to use from *Lord of the Flies*.
- Write your answer.
- Look at the list of key points for each question in the **Answers**.

Character and relationship questions

16. How does Golding present Roger as cruel?

   Write about:

   - the things Roger does and says in the novel
   - how Golding presents Roger by the way he writes.

   [30 marks] AO4 [4 marks]

17. 'Piggy could think.' How far does Golding present Piggy as intelligent?

   Write about:

   - how Piggy speaks and behaves
   - how Golding presents Piggy by the way he writes.

   [30 marks] AO4 [4 marks]

Themes, issues and ideas questions

18. What ideas about religion and belief does Golding explore in *Lord of the Flies*?

   Write about:

   - how the boys express religious ideas and/or different kinds of belief in the novel
   - how Golding presents ideas about religion and belief.

   [30 marks] AO4 [4 marks]

19. 'Maybe it's just us.' How far does Golding present the boys as evil?

   Write about:

   - how different characters are presented as evil
   - how Golding presents the boys as evil by the way he writes.

   [30 marks] AO4 [4 marks]

GLOSSARY

Literary or language terms	Explanation
adjective	a word used to describe something or somebody (the **red** hat)
allegory	a narrative, short story, poem or other work in which the characters or events are symbols that stand for ideas about life or society
antagonist	character who opposes, conflicts with or is the main obstacle to the protagonist, sometimes as simple as 'the villain'
colloquial	the everyday speech used by people in ordinary situations
dialogue	speech and conversation between characters
dramatic irony	when something said by a character is understood with more depth by the audience, sometimes even completely reversing the meaning
foreshadowing	a hint of what is to come in a work of poetry, fiction or drama
imagery	descriptive language that uses images to make actions, objects and characters more vivid in the reader's mind
irony	deliberately saying one thing when you mean another, usually in a humorous, sarcastic or sometimes thoughtful way
metaphor	when one thing is used to describe another to create a striking or unusual image
non-standard English	words, phrases and grammatical forms which fall outside of the standard, conventional form of English
non-standard grammar	constructions which are not considered Standard English, such as non-standard verb agreements like 'we was', 'I've went' or pronoun usage like 'here's me bag'
omniscient narrator	the voice in a novel or other work that is outside the story and appears to know everything and sound reliable
protagonist	the main or a major character
simile	when one thing is compared directly with another using 'like' or 'as'
Standard English	the form of English most widely accepted as the conventional form
subverts	undermines or overturns the conventions of
symbol	something that represents something else, usually with meanings that are widely known (e.g. a dove as a symbol of peace)

ANSWERS

Note that the sample paragraphs given here provide only one possible approach to each task. Many other approaches would also be valid and appropriate.

PLOT AND STRUCTURE

Chapters One and Two – Now you try! (page 7)
The opening chapters introduce the idea of conflict through the presentation of Piggy, who is lecturing the other boys in Chapter Two: 'Like kids!' he said scornfully. 'Acting like a crowd of kids!'. This shows how Piggy is set apart from the others, playing an adult role and scolding them for their childish behaviour. Golding makes it easy for the reader to appreciate why Piggy finds it hard to make friends.

Chapters Three and Four – Now you try! (page 9)
Golding portrays the breaking down of civilisation into savagery soon after the boys' arrival on the island. This can be seen in Chapter Three when Jack tries 'to convey the compulsion to track down and kill that was swallowing him up.' It is clear here that Jack is being overtaken by the desire to hunt and kill. Golding's use of the word 'compulsion' and the phrase 'swallowing him up' shows how helpless Jack is to resist this urge.

Chapters Five and Six – Now you try! (page 11)
Jack and Ralph's growing conflict can also be seen through Golding's exploration of the theme of order. It is presented through Jack's outburst: '"Conch! Conch!" shouted Jack, "we don't need the conch any more. We know who ought to say things."' This shows his growing frustration with Ralph's rules, and with civilisation in general. He wants to ignore the conch's democracy and let only the powerful speak – those who 'ought to say things'.

Chapters Seven and Eight – Now you try! (page 13)
Golding also uses the idea of the beast to show how Simon's character develops. When he communicates with the pig's head/Lord of the Flies, it becomes explicit that he understands more than the other boys: 'Fancy thinking the Beast was something you could hunt and kill!... You knew, didn't you? I'm part of you?' Here Golding shows that Simon has developed the philosophical or spiritual awareness to understand the beast's true nature.

Chapters Nine and Ten – Now you try! (page 15)
A function of Jack's tribe is to represent dictatorships. The idea of the inequality in his camp is explored when Jack tells Ralph 'the conch doesn't count at this end of the island—', showing that in his tribe, his word counts and he gets to decide who speaks. Golding shows Jack dismissing the conch as a symbol of rejecting democracy and also to demonstrate his values.

Chapters Eleven and Twelve – Now you try! (page 17)
The novel's closing chapters make use of some of the symbolism that threads throughout the book. Golding brings back the symbol of the signal fire to contrast Jack and Ralph's styles of leadership. Ralph asks, 'Do you remember how he went hunting and the fire went out and a ship passed by?' As the conch group are at this point unable to light a fire, this shows how savagery has wrecked their attempts at order and rationality.

Form and Structure – Now you try! (page 19)
Golding uses the novel's structure to clearly show the breakdown of order on the island. This is clear when the climax in the form of Piggy's death is reached: 'Piggy's arms and legs twitched a bit, like a pig's after it has been killed', which shows how de-humanised he has become in the eyes of the other boys.

Quick Revision – Quick quiz (pages 20–1)
1 Ralph and Piggy are the first two boys we encounter in the book. 2 Piggy knows how to blow the conch. 3 The first death is the boy with the mulberry birthmark, who dies in the fire. 4 Ralph is angry with Jack because he has been hunting (which he enjoys) when Ralph has been working hard building shelters. 5 The younger boys are scared of a beast, a 'snake-thing'. 6 Simon suggests the beast is 'only us'. 7 *Lord of the Flies* is similar to novels in the adventure genre. 8 Roger throws stones around Henry, but doesn't dare aim them directly at him. 9 Ralph remembers various things, including: wild ponies, cornflakes, books, cars, trains. 10 The hunters leave a pig's head on a stick. 11 The 'Lord of the Flies' is the pig's head left for the beast (it becomes infested with flies, so they seem to be worshipping it). 12 Samneric are frightened by a dead parachutist. 13 Simon is killed by the other boys in the frenzy of a hunting chant. 14 Piggy looks after the littluns. 15 Samneric are forced to join Jack's tribe. 16 The 'confrontation' stage is caused by Jack's breaking away from the group and Ralph's leadership. 17 Jack steals Piggy's glasses. 18 The conch is broken when Piggy is killed. 19 Samneric tell Ralph that he is to be hunted. 20 The naval officer sees the fire lit by Jack.

Quick Revision – Power paragraphs (page 21)
1. Ralph and Piggy's differences are initially shown to be largely physical, as Ralph is fit and a good swimmer but Piggy is fat and has 'ass-mar'. However, as Golding develops their characters, he makes it clear that 'Piggy could think'. This line, delivered through Ralph's thoughts as he prepares for the important assembly, is also significant because it shows how their relationship is progressing as Ralph begins to appreciate Piggy more.

2. Golding includes the scene of Roger throwing stones around Henry, because it shows that civilisation is still influencing Roger at this point. Roger does not dare throw the stones directly at Henry here, because 'Round the squatting child was the protection of parents and school and policemen and the law'. This scene is echoed later in Piggy's death scene, when Roger feels no such limitations, having reached the full extent of his savagery.

Quick Revision – Exam practice (page 21)

- Jack criticises Ralph directly, referring to irrelevant points, showing his beliefs about power: 'He's not a hunter ... He isn't a prefect.'
- Jack uses the boys' fear of the beast to try to break up the group, but is unsuccessful: '"How many think —" His voice tailed off.'

SETTING AND CONTEXT

The shadow of war – Now you try! (page 23)

Views of Western and specifically British identity in the Cold War context are explored by Golding through the novel. For example, when the naval officer rescues the boys, he says, 'I should have thought that a pack of British boys ... would have been able to put up a better show than that —' This reflects beliefs that the British were morally superior to other nationalities and, for example, that Hitler's rise could not have happened in Britain.

Education and adventure – Now you try! (page 25)

The context of the boys' education is used by Golding to support the novel's themes. This is seen when Jack argues his case for leadership by stating 'I can sing C sharp'. This skill, that was prized at school, is inappropriate for leadership on the island, but it also highlights his skill as a chorister, which encourages the reader to interpret him as innocent. This emphasises the theme of good and evil, as Golding highlights the purity of the schoolboys by making some of them (the most violent, in fact) choirboys.

Quick revision – Quick quiz (page 27)

1 The Eastern Bloc, led by the USSR, and the West, led by the US, were involved in the Cold War. 2 Books in the adventure genre include: Treasure Island, Swallows and Amazons, The Coral Island. 3 The boys swim in the lagoon/the pool. 4 Children who were academic went to a grammar school. 5 An atom bomb is a highly destructive, nuclear, weapon. 6 The Cold War encouraged black and white thinking, for example that people and ideas were either 'good' or 'bad'. 7 The conch group end up in the huts by the platform. 8 Golding did not feel glad to be British because he had seen British soldiers behave just as badly as German ones. 9 Most of the hunting takes place in the forest. 10 The aspects of school routine that are most relevant are: strict rules, discipline and talking in turn.

Quick revision – Power paragraphs (page 27)

- Two sides – East/West, dictatorship/democracy – are reflected in Jack and Ralph; democracy shown as civilised solution and communism makes tempting offer ('we hunt and feast and have fun') but is savage
- Bomb is reason boys are on island – 'they're all dead' – first thing they do is try to build a civilised society ('hands up like at school')

CHARACTERS

Ralph – Now you try! (page 29)

Golding shows how Ralph develops as a representative for civilisation in the novel by showing how he can plan for the future, which is a civilised (rather than primitive or savage) trait. This is clear from early on, for example when he argues with Jack, shouting 'Don't you want to be rescued? All you can talk about is pig, pig, pig!', which highlights the separation in their interests, and therefore their values.

Jack – Now you try! (page 31)

Golding uses Jack to contribute to the novel's presentation of savagery by introducing the primitive form of religion through the offering he makes: 'This head is for the beast. It's a gift.' This shows faith in a magical form of pre-Christian spirituality, where leaving 'gifts' for a supernatural being keeps the population safe. Golding does this to demonstrate Jack's regression out of civilisation into savagery.

Piggy – Now you try! (page 33)

Golding shows how Piggy represents logic and is linked to the theme of civilisation in his approach to the problem of the signal fire: 'We could experiment. We could find out how to make a small hot fire and then put green branches on to make smoke.' This shows how Piggy uses rationality and logic to problem-solve, associating him with civilisation rather than savagery, as his approach is always to think first before acting.

Simon – Now you try! (page 35)

Golding presents Simon as having greater understanding than the other boys when they discuss the nature of the beast. However, he struggles to express this in a way that they will understand: 'What is the dirtiest thing there is?' He is talking about the nature of evil itself, but Jack interprets this crudely and the other boys are happy to join Jack in laughing at Simon, who they perceive as 'batty'.

Roger – Now you try! (page 37)

Golding shows how Roger gives way to savagery when the hunters track the sow with piglets: 'One piglet, with a demented shriek, rushed into the sea trailing Roger's spear behind it.' If the hunters were sensible, they would not pursue a sow as she and her piglets could produce future meat. Golding is showing how the hunters display the lack of thought typical of savagery.

ANSWERS

Sam and Eric – Now you try! (page 39)

Samneric's role in the novel develops as they come to represent ordinary people. This is apparent when they give Ralph practical advice at the end: 'Listen Ralph, never mind what's sense. That's gone.' They can recognise how absurd things have become, but they are unable to give Ralph practical help because it is not safe for them to do so. This shows their lack of power.

The littluns – Now you try! (page 41)

Golding uses the littluns to show the effects of key themes such as fear, for example when a meeting is called to report the sighting of the beast: 'the littluns whimpered as now they so frequently did'. As the smallest and most vulnerable of the boys, it is the littluns who often bear the brunt of 'things break[ing] up' – the first to die is a littlun and many of them have nightmares.

Quick revision – Quick quiz (pages 42–3)

1 Jack has red hair. 2 Ralph represents democracy. 3 Simon is 'batty'. 4 Roger and Maurice kick over littluns' sandcastles. 5 Jack's last name is Merridew. 6 Percival Wemys Madison is the other character whose full name we know. 7 Roger kills Piggy. 8 Ralph weeps 'for the end of innocence'. 9 Jack paints his face. 10 Possible littluns names include: Henry, Percival, Johnny, Phil. 11 Jack leaves an offering for the beast. 12 Ralph, Jack, Piggy, Simon, Sam and Eric are in the 'conch group'. 13 Simon picks fruit for littluns. 14 The littluns fall off the log at assemblies. 15 Piggy knows how to blow the conch. 16 Sam and Eric are twins. 17 Piggy 'could think'. 18 Simon talks to the Lord of the Flies. 19 The boy with the mulberry birthmark is the first to die. 20 Jack represents dictator-style power, like communism.

Quick revision – Power paragraphs (page 43)

1. Golding presents Jack as caught up by the hunt from early in the novel. When Ralph is angry with Jack for not helping to build shelters, Jack 'trie[s] to convey the compulsion to track down and kill that was swallowing him up.' Golding uses 'swallowing' as a metaphor to show how powerless Jack feels against this desire, as well as the verb 'trie[s]' to show his inability to express how he feels.
2. Percival Wemys Madison first appears at the assembly 'to decide about the fear', where he is asked his name, which he recites along with his address and then bursts into tears, having got stuck on the telephone number. Later, when the boys are found, he 'sought in his head for an incantation that had faded clean away'. Golding uses Percival to show the erosion of civilisation, as he gradually loses this well-memorised piece of information.

Quick revision – Exam practice (page 43)

• Jack's arrogance and stubbornness, bullying nature; belief in immediate concerns (food/meat/hunting) as more important; refusal to apologise fully ('I'm sorry. About the fire, I mean.')

• Ralph's shift in loyalties – 'a link between him and Jack had been snapped and fastened elsewhere'; Simon's sympathy with Piggy, giving him meat.

THEMES

Good and evil – Now you try! (page 45)

Golding shows that good is only apparent in the earlier parts of the novel and in very few characters. For example, Simon's goodness is shown in small kindnesses, such as helping the littluns in the forest: 'Simon found for them the fruit they could not reach', and in his attempts to tell the boys about the beast. Simon, as the only one with no blood on his hands, is the only pure character.

Civilisation and savagery – Now you try! (page 47)

Golding explores the ease with which boys slip from a civilised state to a state of savagery. An example that suggests the boys enjoy descending into savagery comes when Jack paints his face. Golding states: 'the mask was a thing on its own, behind which Jack hid, liberated from shame and self-consciousness', which paints this experience positively. The verb 'liberated' shows that Jack is discovering his true, savage, self.

Power and leadership – Now you try! (page 49)

Golding uses Ralph and Jack to present opposing ideas about leadership. This is clear when Ralph solemnly prepares for the meeting after the fire has been let out and the ship was missed: 'This meeting must not be fun, but business.' Later, when Jack leads his own group, he will emphasise 'fun' as the aim of his tribe. Golding shows here how Ralph is aware of the responsibilities of leadership, and wants to do a good job.

Fear and the beast – Now you try! (page 51)

Golding uses the beast to highlight differences between the characters, as they respond differently to it. This is clear when Ralph responds, 'You couldn't have a beastie, a snake-thing, on an island this size.' True to his nature, Ralph's immediate response to the littluns' fear is practical and logical. Golding offers an argument against the beast's existence while also strengthening Ralph's characterisation as a sensible, practical individual.

Friendship – Now you try! (page 53)

Golding shows how Ralph and Piggy's friendship develops through the novel, based on shared experiences and values that they have in common. For example, when Jack begins to threaten the group, Piggy points out: 'He can't hurt you: but if you stand out of the way he'd hurt the next thing.' This shows that Jack associates Ralph and Piggy together, because of their shared devotion to the conch, i.e. loyalty to democratic values.

Nature and religion – Now you try! (page 55)

Golding portrays the boys acting on belief in different ways in the novel, using the idea of religion

ANSWERS

to highlight their characters and their descent into savagery. For example, Ralph's wish 'If only they could send us something grown-up … a sign or something' brings the parachutist to the island. Golding here shows how grown-ups are unfit to answer Ralph's innocent childish hopes, as their war-torn world is no better than the island.

Quick revision – Quick quiz (pages 56–7)

1 The symbols of civilisation are the conch, the signal fire and Piggy's glasses (and Ralph and Piggy). 2 The boys are scared of the beast. 3 The signal fire is important for the themes of civilisation, leadership, and the beast (to an extent). 4 Simon says **'maybe it's only us'**. 5 The power struggles are between Jack and Ralph. 6 The huts offer protection from the elements and show long-term planning. Only a civilised society would bother to make them. 7 Simon is shown engaging in a form of meditation, Ralph makes a kind of wish for a sign, and the savages make a primitive offering under Jack's direction. 8 The Lord of the Flies is the pig's head left as an offering. 9 Ralph represents democratically-elected leadership. 10 Samneric think the parachutist is the beast. 11 It matters that the hunters kill a sow with piglets because it's wasteful – leaving the piglets to grow up would mean a supply of meat into the future. 12 Jack introduces the mask. 13 The mask represents savagery. 14 The quotation refers to Ralph's friendship/loyalty transferring from Jack to Piggy. 15 Piggy is killed along with the conch, showing how closely the two are linked – Piggy finds the conch and has the most faith in it. 16 Simon is the most 'good'. 17 Ralph leaves Jack's friendship behind for Piggy's. 18 It is significant that Roger throws stones 'to miss' Henry because at this point he is still governed by civilisation. 19 Jack represents dictatorship/totalitarianism (e.g. fascism, communism). 20 Leaving the pig's head out for the beast is an act of savagery, a primitive form of religion. Also, the conversation the pig's head has with Simon stresses the theme of savagery.

Quick revision – Power paragraphs (page 57)

1. Initially, the boys intend to organise themselves in an orderly way. Even Jack at first says 'We've got to have rules and obey them.' With practical Ralph in charge, they make sensible rules that will make their lives easier, like controlling toileting. They also copy familiar rules: 'We'll have to have 'Hands up' like at school.' Golding shows how the boys are influenced by the civilisation they know.
2. Golding uses the natural world to highlight the theme of evil in the scene where Simon is killed. He describes the storm in a way that creates tension which seems to drive the boys into violence, as they are too savage to separate from nature at this point: 'The flickering light became brighter and the blows of the thunder were only just bearable.' The natural world emphasises and drives the boys' evil.

Quick revision – Exam practice (page 57)

- 'Fancy thinking the beast was something you could hunt and kill!': this portrays the beast not as physical, but as inside the boys – and shows Simon was right in his earlier comments about the beast and nature of evil.
- 'You don't want Ralph to think you're batty, do you?': clear sense of a warning, with Simon being told not to tell or the others won't like him, so friendship presented as risky/something to bargain for (also link to Simon as prophet – never believed).

LANGUAGE

Voice and dialogue – Now you try! (page 59)

Golding uses the third person omniscient narrative voice to support thematic ideas even when describing actions and setting. For example, when the boys were hunting, their 'footsteps and the occasional breeze were stirring up small devils of dust'. Here, Golding uses the metaphor 'devils of dust' to create connotations of evil around the beast.

Writer's effects – Now you try! (page 61)

Golding chooses language features to support the allegorical meanings created in the novel. For example, when Jack attacks Ralph's group, Piggy fails to protect his glasses, because he 'thought they wanted the conch'. Golding reminds the reader of the conch's importance for Piggy, because it stands for democracy, organised assemblies and being civilised – none of which ever mattered to Jack. The glasses, representing Piggy's metaphorical clear-sightedness, only matter to Jack as tools to light fire.

EXAM PRACTICE

Planning your character response – Now you try! (page 67)

- Paragraph 1: Ralph shown as brave at the start: diving into the pool; Piggy admires him.
- Paragraph 2: 'I'm chief. I'll go.' – Ralph goes ahead when hunting the beast, and even Jack is scared. Golding shows him as brave by not letting others argue.
- Paragraph 3: Ralph nervous before big assembly but faces it: 'I can't think, not like Piggy'.
- Paragraph 4: Goes to confront Jack after stealing Piggy's glasses, wants to face him clean: 'we won't be painted … because we aren't savages'.
- Paragraph 5: Only one to face naval officer – because only one left with some civilisation/humanity; officer embarrassed that Ralph weeps, but strength of his emotion indicates bravery, shows what he has faced.

Grade 5 answer – Check the skills (page 69)

Points: A key moment that shows Jack's destructiveness is Piggy's death; celebrating that 'The conch is gone'; Jack immediately viciously attacks Ralph by throwing a spear at him; Golding uses Jack

85

ANSWERS

to show destructiveness as both savage and wasteful; Jack's destructive nature and savagery prevents him from planning ahead and thinking logically like Piggy, which leads him and his hunters to kill a sow with piglets; he sets fire to the entire forest just to force Ralph out to catch him, destroying all the fruit trees and wildlife.

Context: Jack's role as a symbol for dictatorships like nazism or communism

Interpretations: Golding shows us how much Jack hates the conch, as a symbol of democracy, through this celebration of its destruction; he is now freed to attack people; his destructiveness has turned towards humans; killing the sow and piglets shows thoughtlessness, as future meat is also being destroyed; Jack's destructive attitude is wasteful and pointless.

Grade 5 answer – Now you try! (page 69)

Jack's main conflict through the book is with Ralph, from when Jack 'let the bloody fire out'. Jack wants to be chief and he tries to win support several times, for example with 'Who thinks Ralph oughtn't to be chief?' after they've seen the parachutist. This demonstrates how he is destructive and wants to break up the group by trying to get other boys to follow him. Also, by constantly emphasising 'my hunters', using the possessive 'my' because these are the only boys who follow him unquestioningly, it prevents the boys feeling united, as it highlights the hunters as a separate group.

Grade 7+ answer – Check the skills (page 71)

Points: Golding focuses Jack's attention on the conch's destruction rather than on Piggy's death to highlight the symbolism of this moment; Jack has hated the conch for a large part of the novel, declaring it 'doesn't count' in different parts of the island and mocking Ralph and Piggy's devotion to it; Golding uses Jack to show how wasteful and savage destructiveness is. This is clearest through the depletion of natural resources: the sow and the burnt-up forest.

Context: As Jack represents totalitarian leadership which, to Golding's contemporary readers would resonate most strongly as Stalin or Hitler, his joy at the destruction of a symbol of democracy works on the allegorical level to highlight the conflict between him and Ralph as symbols of different systems.

Interpretations: Jack's focus on 'fun' is shown to be in conflict with Ralph's focus on preparedness.

Grade 7+ answer – Now you try! (page 71)

AO1

- Ralph is physically brave at the start of the novel: diving, swimming and heading off to explore without hesitation.
- Ralph is confident enough to address a crowd of strange boys.
- Ralph goes ahead, while even Jack is scared when they go to hunt the beast.
- Ralph is the only one with the moral courage to accept responsibility for Simon's death (even if he does then talk himself out of it, arguably for Piggy's sake).

AO2

- Golding uses Ralph to represent rationality and democracy, which he intends the reader to see as braver choices than savagery and giving into the 'fun' of short-termism.
- Ralph's language shows bravery in his struggle to hold on to humanity and civilisation in the face of barbarism: 'I'd like to put on war paint and be a savage. But we must keep the fire burning. The fire's the most important thing on the island, because, because —'
- Use of first person to show personal responsibility: 'I'm chief. I'll go.'
- Ralph 'wept for the end of innocence, the darkness of man's heart and the fall through the air of the true, wise friend called Piggy' – list of three to emphasise how much Ralph has to face.

AO3

- Ralph's representation of democracy is a braver option than savagery and seeking the promises of 'fun' and 'feasting' offered by communism/fascism, as represented by Jack.
- Ralph is closer than most to the hero of the typical adventure novel, as he retains a lot of his civilisation and acts like a classic explorer.

Planning your theme response – Now you try! (page 75)

- Paragraph 1: Fear emerges at the second meeting – 'snake-thing'; laughed at by older ones; dismissed as just littluns; 'couldn't have a beastie, a snake-thing, on an island this size'.
- Paragraph 2: Fear to highlight rational versus irrational (savage) approach – Ralph versus Jack: 'we'd hunt and kill it', and later encourages fear to drive boys to his group.
- Paragraph 3: Piggy's fear – of people, especially Jack – logical fear, 'he hates me'.
- Paragraph 4: Simon – Lord of the Flies threatens him with loss of friends.
- Paragraph 5: Boys should be scared of each other – the only violence comes from them.

Grade 5 answer – Check the skills (page 77)

Points: Safety and protection (Golding shows that having a civilised way of running things gives the boys the best chance of survival. The less civilised and more savage they become, they more danger they are in, and the less chance of rescue they have); The way the novel ends makes clear how far from civilisation the boys have come (The naval officer represents the civilised world coming back to rescue them – Golding uses him to show that the boys have got too savage to help themselves. Most of them are too far gone to even speak to him as they have left order so far behind. Jack tries to come forward, but stops himself and Percival Wemys Madison has forgotten even his personal details that earlier he was repeating like a chant.)

Context: Civilised (or democratic) society is safer than a savage (or communist) one.

Interpretations: I think Golding wants the reader to see that if they all kept their roles, so Jack didn't 'let the bloody fire out', they would have been rescued much sooner; This shows that order is what could keep them safe, showing that a civilised (or democratic) society is safer than a savage (or communist) one.

Grade 5 answer – Now you try! (page 77)

Golding uses the novel's language to show how order breaks down. At the start, there are 'little 'uns', but by the end, the words have been pushed together to say 'littluns', so even the boundaries between words are breaking up. A similar thing happens to the twins' names, Sam and Eric, which become Samneric. Jack's tribe shows this too, as the boys are called 'savages' and the chant they do uses simple, short words to create a strong rhythm: 'Kill the beast! Cut his throat! Spill his blood!' Golding's descriptive language is often rich and complex, especially at the start, for example with the description of 'efflorescence of tropical weed and coral', so this simplicity of language as the boys become more savage is very significant.

Grade 7+ answer – Check the skills (page 79)

Points: Golding demonstrates that running things in a civilised way makes life safer for the boys; Ironically, of course, it is this final savage fire that brings the naval officer to the island, but Golding shows that Ralph is the only boy left with enough civilisation to speak to an outsider.
Context: The book reflects Golding's experiences of people's attitudes to Britishness.
Interpretations: Golding uses fire as a symbol to contrast civilisation and savagery. (The signal fire is fire in its civilised form. Savage fire also exists, for example when it burns out of control at the start of the novel, and when Jack smokes Ralph out at the end.); The naval officer functions as a new civilised lens to view the 'group of painted boys' through, as the reader has been immersed in their experiences. His external judgement that a 'pack of British boys' should have 'put up a better show', shows how far from civilisation the boys have come.

Grade 7+ answer – Now you try! (page 79)

AO1
- Fear and the beast link to the theme of evil.
- Simon recognises that the boys are the evil and do not need to fear the beast.
- Piggy says there's only people to be scared of; Jack scolds the littluns for their fear.
- Ralph is rational and reassuring: 'you couldn't have a beastie, a snake-thing, on an island this size.'

AO2
- Golding uses the symbol of the beast to explore the characters' motivations and true natures.
- Fear comes up in multiple assemblies, until Ralph says they must 'decide there's nothing in it' – tries to get rid of it with rational discussion.
- 'Of course we're frightened sometimes' – Jack presents fear as an expected, normal thing ('of course') but says they must 'put up with' it.

- Fear builds for the boys with the beast talk, but Golding creates tension through the boys' actions, building more quickly from Simon's death as the violence increases.

AO3
- The boys' presumed evacuation from war adds irony (as they are not safe), and would be a more obvious circumstance to a contemporary audience due to their own recent wartime experience or the Cold War context.
- Fear is in keeping with the adventure novel genre, where external dangers are the only problems the boys face, such as wild beasts, savages, natural disaster.

Practice questions – Question 16

AO1
- Roger's cruelty develops as he becomes increasingly freed from civilisation.
- Roger admires Jack's use of violent defences for the tribe.
- It is Roger who kills Piggy and tortures the twins.
- Roger is described as 'a terror' by Samneric.

AO2
- Roger is primarily associated with acts of cruelty and violence; Golding does not present him engaging in normal activity.
- 'Roger led the way straight through the castles' – Golding shows how Roger intentionally spoils the littluns' games.
- 'with a sense of delirious abandonment' – Golding presents killing Piggy as a joyful act for Roger.
- 'Roger's sharpened a stick at both ends' – Golding presents Roger as treating Ralph as prey.

AO3
- In the political allegory, Roger represents figures or institutions that carry out violence on behalf of the leader or regime.
- Roger's natural sadism emerges easily, but could be shocking to adults who had not, like Golding, worked in schools (especially the intense atmosphere of 1940s/50s boarding schools).

Practice questions – Question 17

AO1
- It is Piggy who knows what to do with the conch, and continues to see it as a valuable asset.
- Piggy lacks social/emotional intelligence; he does not approach other people in the best way ('Like a pack of kids!').
- Piggy wants to construct things such as sundials.
- Piggy reminds Ralph of the importance of the signal fire towards the end, when he keeps forgetting.

AO2
- Golding uses Piggy as a symbol of logic and rationality.
- Piggy is closest to an adult view because of how he sees the world: 'What's grown-ups goin' to think?'

ANSWERS

- Golding shows Piggy's intelligence through other characters: 'Piggy could think.' (Ralph's perspective)
- Golding shows Piggy as hardly changing from his initial civilised state, for example his hair doesn't grow – but even he is caught up in Simon's death dance, and cannot admit it: 'you and I was only on the outside'.

AO3

- Piggy's intellect helps Golding make a case for democracy as superior to dictatorship, since democracy is shown as supported by the more rational characters.
- At the start, Piggy is reminiscent of comic characters like Billy Bunter, being fat and socially awkward.

Practice questions – Question 18

AO1

- Simon seeks solitude to commune with the forest in a kind of meditation.
- Ralph makes a kind of wish for a sign from the world of the grown-ups, which is answered with the arrival of the dead parachutist.
- The hunting dance and chant is ritualistic and similar to some religious practices.
- Jack decides that part of each kill will be left for the beast.

AO2

- Golding's description of Simon's clearing is lush and vibrant, with his 'candle-buds' and 'screen of leaves' invoking peace and connotations of worship.
- 'Kill the beast! Cut his throat! Spill his blood!': the rhythm created by monosyllabic words in threes sounds like drumming.
- The symbol of the dead parachutist, mistaken for the beast but really a 'poor broken thing', shows how little the boys can rely on the outside world for answers.
- Religious imagery and symbolism present Simon as a Christ-like figure, martyred when the boys cannot understand his message.

AO3

- The offering to the beast is reminiscent of ancient religious practice, like leaving tributes for gods to avoid harm.
- Simon is like Christ because he: spends time alone in meditation; is taunted by the devil/demon pig's head; is not believed when he conveys his message. Even after death he has a halo of light made by sea creatures that makes him look more holy.

Practice questions – Question 19

AO1

- None of the problems the boys face are anything but their own making.
- Roger starts by teasing littluns and ends with murder and torture.
- Jack hits Piggy and won't apologise, and seeks to break up the group multiple times.
- Not all the boys are evil, but even Ralph and Piggy are involved in the 'murder' of Simon, and cannot fully admit to it – Piggy not at all, and Ralph not for long.

AO2

- The choir is introduced as 'something dark', foreshadowing their position as the most wicked.
- 'Maybe it's just us': the beast as a symbol for evil, and as evil within the boys.
- The evil develops throughout the novel, influenced by time away from civilisation/adult supervision/rule of law.
- Difficulties in naming evil shown through a vagueness in language, e.g. 'something dark', 'maybe it's just us'/'what's the dirtiest thing there is?', 'it wasn't – what you said'.

AO3

- Golding's intentions with the novel included showing evil as a normal part of human nature: 'man produces evil as a bee produces honey'.
- Golding's war experiences influenced him, as many people were relieved to be British after the Second World War because they could be proud to 'not have been Nazis'. Golding recognised that there had been atrocities on all sides.